VICTORIAN
FURNITURE AND FURNISHINGS

The Victorians were prolific producers of things. For instance, it has been estimated that in the six decades of Queen Victoria's reign more furniture was produced than in all the previous centuries put together. No doubt the same holds true for the other forms of applied art. So much so, indeed, that merely to give a catalogue of the names of the objects made would take up most of the space available. A considerable degree of selectivity is, therefore, inevitable.

The method adopted is to strike a balance between what is available, what is fashionable at the present moment and what is of permanent worth. In the last case, except for one or two instances where the author feels that past fashion has been confused with genuine objective worth, he has allowed his own personal preferences to be overriden by expert consensus.

The author also wishes to acknowledge his debt to Claud Birt Jennings for his generous help and advice.

A
GROSSET
ALL-COLOR GUIDE

VICTORIAN
FURNITURE AND FURNISHINGS

BY JÜRI GABRIEL
Illustrated by Peter Morter & Design Bureau

GROSSET & DUNLAP
A NATIONAL GENERAL COMPANY
Publishers · New York

THE GROSSET ALL-COLOR GUIDE SERIES
SUPERVISING EDITOR ... GEORG ZAPPLER
Board of Consultants

CONTENTS

VICTORIANA

Though art is a fluid process, and as such is not bound by the life and death cycle of monarchy, one cannot help feeling that the Prince Regent provided something of an exception to this rule. When George IV died in 1830, the Regency spirit died with him. By the time Victoria came to the throne, though furniture—to take but one form of applied art—had changed relatively little in outward appearance, the mood it created was different. Regency furniture, even at its most exaggerated, had an air of gaiety and that particular easy elegance one senses in people who are certain of their own taste.

The new early Victorian middle class lacked this certainty. It had not had the benefit of the aesthetic hothouse of inherited wealth nor was its earned income sufficient to indulge in

Goss parian bust of
Queen Victoria, 1887

Mahogany chair, c. 1820

Mahogany chair, c. 1835

the Georgian hobby of individual patronage. What the average middle-class client wanted was value for money, and so, instead of commissioning something to meet his specific needs, he chose, in a shop, what he liked best from a range of items produced 'on spec'. Thus aesthetic judgment became the affair of the commercially efficient manufacturer, often the person least equipped to be an arbiter of taste.

The result was conservatism; partly because the manufacturer saw no real reason to go to the expense of radically new designs while his main market remained aesthetically uncommitted, and partly because new designs often involved pay disputes. Whereas the *London Cabinet-Makers Union Book of Rules* gave agreed rates of pay for existing designs, the establishment of a similar scale for any new design could, and often did, involve time-consuming negotiation.

Yet, in spite of this innate conservatism, the Regency style was gradually superseded as a result of natural stylistic evolution (few manufacturers can resist the temptation of slightly 'im-

5

(*right*) Elaborate table center with ruby trailing by Hodgetts, Richardson & Son, Stourbridge, c. 1878

(*far right*) Silver candlesticks made for Liberty & Co., 1906-07. The original design by R. Silver was commissioned in 1900

Multi-columned card table with inlaid walnut top, c. 1860

proving' even a good design, especially if it increases their profit margin by reducing costs). An additional cause was the growing belief in the moral purpose of art (one of the main effects of the Victorian religious revival); it was felt that the immorality of the Regency period tainted its art as well. The opinions of Augustus Welby Pugin (architect, designer and critic) on architecture, which directly inspired the Gothic Revival, and Prince Albert's abandonment of the Brighton Pavilion show us how this moralistic attitude affected the Victorian view of art in general. They also help to explain why Wilde's and Whistler's doctrine of 'art for art's sake' was considered so revolutionary.

However, as we have already remarked, the counter-force of conservativism prevented immediate wholesale rejection of values, and furniture, costume, indeed applied art in general, retained enough of the characteristics of the late Regency style to be often described as 'Regency fattened-up'. A telling phrase, for the very process of fattening up, the rounding-off

of angles and the increasing use of sprung upholstery in furniture, tended to destroy the essential Regency characteristic of proportion.

Even more disruptive was the Victorian attitude to ornamentation. Whatever decoration Regency craftsmen used, it remained decoration, and an object still relied on its good proportions for its effect. For the Victorians, however, design came to be equated more and more with ornament. Despite the efforts of critics like Pugin, this trend continued with increasing emphasis on elaboration for its own sake until, toward the latter part of the nineteenth century, the quest for prestige ended in mere bombast. When the inevitable reaction took place, the unadventurous opted for a weak revival of eighteenth-century designs, but their more daring brothers gradually began to replace art based on the past with the art of the present: Art Nouveau, which at its best was remarkably successful in its aim of synthesis of form and decoration in one complete organic unity.

Furniture

In spite of the appalling conditions in which the working class had to live in the nineteenth century, this period saw a dramatic increase in both the population and the overall wealth of the country. For the furniture industry, as for every other industry, this meant two things: an ever-expanding market on the one hand, and ever-increasing competition from rival manufacturers on the other. In the mad scramble to reduce prices, substitutes were found for expensive materials (Muntz metal replaced ormolu, and cheaper woods were hand-painted to imitate the more expensive ones) and, from the late 1860's onward, the already low labor costs were further reduced by the expanded use of machines.

The influence of mechanization of the Victorian furniture

Beech chair stained to resemble rosewood, 1840. The shape is a common variant of the balloon-back.

Mid- to late Victorian machine-carved bedside cabinet

industry is almost always exaggerated. Although nearly all the most important wood-working machines had been invented by 1837, they were not widely used before the 1870's. Until the mid-Victorian period, the bulk of the trade still consisted of small family businesses which, as economic units, were simply not large enough to benefit from the capital expenditure involved in installing such machines—quite apart from the fact that a series of independent reports had flatly rejected wood-working machines as being more expensive than traditional methods (a sad comment on a craftsman's real wages).

The mid-Victorian manufacturer, on the other hand, was helped in his choice not only by the greater size of the economic units (some firms had up to 1,000 employees), but also by the increased demand due to the rapid expansion of the export market resulting from England's new status as world leader in the art of cabinet-making.

The machines themselves fall into two categories: those that merely cut costs without necessarily adversely affecting the workmanship of the final product, and those that sometimes led, either directly or indirectly, to the lowering of standards. In the first category there were the mechanical saws, planing and mortising machines; in the second, the chief culprits were the patent carving machines and the new veneer peeling machine.

In itself the veneer machine was an excellent development, but by making the process so much cheaper, it allowed the unscrupulous manufacturer to use it more for disguising badly constructed pieces than for the decorative purposes for which it was intended. Similarly, there was nothing intrinsically wrong with mechanical carving, as long as the process was not used in a misguided attempt to duplicate the intricacies of elaborate hand-carving.

Yet in spite of these dangers, the craftsmanship of Victorian furniture is excellent (apparently one of the give-aways of late Victorian copies of eighteenth-century pieces is that the workmanship is sometimes too good!). The standard of the plain veneer work is particularly high, as can readily be seen from a comparison with French furniture of the same period.

Although some knowledge of techniques provides a useful background, the study of Victorian furniture is essentially the study of styles. According to Loudon's *Encyclopaedia of Cottage, Farm and Villa Architecture* the four most popular ones in 1833 were: 'the Grecian or modern style [characterized by acanthus leaves] which is by far the most prevalent, the Gothic or Perpendicular style, which imitates the lines and angles of the Tudor Gothic architecture; the Elizabethan style, which combined the Gothic with the Roman or Italian manner; and the style of the age of Louis XIV [virtually interchangeable with Louis XV as fas as the trade was concerned], or the florid Italian, which is characterized by curved lines and excess of curvilinear ornaments.'

The Elizabethan style usually ranged somewhat uneasily between adaptations of basic Carolean and Jacobean shapes and the mere use of strapwork decoration. But whatever its derivation, it fitted the baronial mood of the Romantic literature of the day and the strong feeling held by many people (see Pugin's *Contrasts*) that England ought to seek inspiration in its own divinely ordained past rather than in that of other nations.

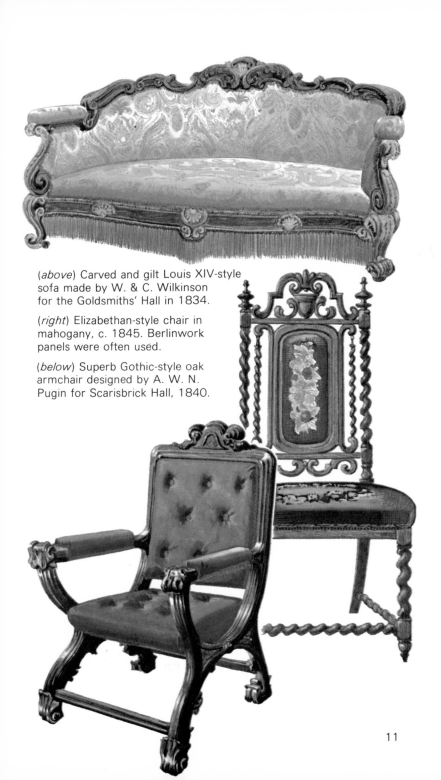

(*above*) Carved and gilt Louis XIV-style sofa made by W. & C. Wilkinson for the Goldsmiths' Hall in 1834.

(*right*) Elizabethan-style chair in mahogany, c. 1845. Berlinwork panels were often used.

(*below*) Superb Gothic-style oak armchair designed by A. W. N. Pugin for Scarisbrick Hall, 1840.

Victorian copy of late
17th-century daybed

As if this multiplicity is not confusing enough, manufacturers began to invent all kinds of new styles which were no nearer in historical terms to what they purported to be than a pedestal sideboard with strapwork decoration is Elizabethan. It quickly became apparent that the style of an item of furniture tended to refer more to the type of decoration that was applied to a basic standard shape than to any real attempt to copy a historical antecedent. But there were exceptions. Notice the illustration above showing a perfect Victorian reproduction of a late seventeenth-century daybed.

In spite of the apparent freedom of the attitude to decoration, early Victorian furniture itself is remarkably restrained. There is no marquetry, inlaid brass or ormolu; even the use of contrasting woods is extremely rare. What makes much of it, especially that of the 1840's, unpleasing to the eye is not excessive decoration, but its general air of comfortable overstuffed flabbiness. The 1840's, indeed, were one of the rare periods in which comfort, with particular emphasis on the use of upholstery, was preferred to elegance. Easy chairs, sofas and ottomans were smothered with it, apart from their four minute legs (and ottomans did not even have these). Within a decade, though, elegance was once again the prime requisite.

The immediate causes of this temporary fixation with comfort were the decrease in the price of good-quality furnishing fabrics and the increasing use of the coiled spring in upholstery. The latter has often been put forward as the main reason for this development, but furniture-makers had known about the coiled spring for some years (it was patented in 1828) without making much use of it. Far more important, as Peter Floud has pointed out (see his Victoria and Albert Museum publication), was the decrease in the cost of upholstery fabrics resulting from the mechanization of the weaving industry.

In the late 1830's and the 1840's the Grecian was still the most popular style with the trade, but the Old French and the Elizabethan (the so-called François I was often virtually identical) were closing the gap. The position of Gothic, however, was more ambiguous. As a result of the Gothic Revival in church architecture, Gothic became asso-

Heavily upholstered mid-Victorian mahogany dining chair with much-coarsened 18th-century French overtones.

Gothic-style cabinet of painted and carved oak, designed by Pugin and exhibited in the Medieval Court of the Great Exhibition in 1851.

ciated in people's minds with religion and was invested with too much dignity to be freely used for regular furniture.

When one thinks of Gothic, one cannot help thinking of Pugin who, apart from his activities as an architect, was one of the very small number of early Victorian designers remembered by history. His influence on the furniture trade was enormous, but not, for the most part, of the kind he wanted. The bulk of Pugin's designs are simple and restrained, but the publicity given to his few more complicated pieces, like those for the Medieval Court of the Great Exhibition, unfortunately encouraged the trade to indulge its passion for those selfsame creations covered with inappropriate Gothic trimming that Pugin spent so much time denouncing in his critical writings.

The Great Exhibition was held in 1851. Among the Queen's favorite exhibits were *tableaux morts* of stuffed and clothed squirrels, and the furniture section included that essential of life—a dressing table and fire escape combined.

All too often in the past, articles on Victorian furniture

Detail of the elaborately carved Chevy Chase sideboard, made between 1857 and 1863 by Gerrard Robinson of Newcastle.

have been illustrated by engravings from the official catalogue, which has conditioned us to think that the Great Exhibition was truly representative. This is not so; many of the exhibits, including that dressing table, were no more representative of ordinary everyday early Victorian furniture than the mink-covered bed is of today's, but were really the most exaggerated forms of the styles we have already mentioned, as well as a mass of others synthesized by inventive manufacturers. The main object of the exercise then as now was to catch the public's eye, and few exhibits were quite as successful in this as a pair of Irish bog oak chairs covered with extraordinarily elaborate naturalistic carving. As Anthony Bird has pointed out in his *Early Victorian Furniture,* what made these doubly attractive to the average Victorian visitor was the fact that bog oak is almost impossible to carve. Not everything at the Exhibition was so ponderous. Sideboards in the French style, for instance, with their crestings and curves, have a certain appeal and can look marvelous in a modern interior.

The bog oak school of naturalistic carving continued for a number of years after the Exhibition, and occasionally it produced furniture of enormous charm. Regrettably, the work of craftsmen like William Kendall of Warwick, whose technical ability was accompanied by taste, was far outnumbered by that of lesser men, who were never content until every vertical surface of their sideboards dripped with sickly narrative sculpture.

One danger with a summary as brief as this is that by recording the stylistic changes that did take place, one tends to give a false impression of constant flux even to an essentially static period like the years 1830 to 1860. To put early Victorian furniture as a whole into true perspective, one should remember that Thomas King's *The Modern Style*

Elaborate, yet elegant, naturalistic sideboard designed and carved by William Kendall of Warwick in 1858

of *Cabinet Work Exemplified,* published in 1829, was reprinted in 1862 without alteration.

The 1860's and 1870's, in direct contrast, were a period of revolution in the history of furniture design, but all too often the changes that took place are glibly dismissed as symptomatic of the so-called typical Victorian desire for innovation for its own sake. I believe that from the late 1860's onward, Victorian concern with aesthetics was much closer to a search for religious truth than to the dilettantism implied in 'a desire for innovation for its own sake'.

By the same token, if we think of the aesthetic innovators as prophets, we get a truer insight into the impact of their theories. What confuses the issue, however, are the numerous discrepancies between aesthetic theories and actual practice: between William Burges' advocation of simplicity in design on the one hand and the overly elaborate decoration of his own house on the other.

Just how much aesthetic innovators like Charles Eastlake, first director of the National Gallery, altered the whole balance of the furniture industry can only be appreciated by comparing the attitude of the pre-1860's public to furniture styles with that of the later Victorians.

For the first half of the Victorian period the four major styles, Grecian, French, Elizabethan and Gothic, enjoyed virtually equal status. There was an understandable bias toward the use of masculine styles, like the Elizabethan, for masculine environments such as the library and, equally, of the more delicate French style for female spheres of influence. But these pressures only really affected the rich whose houses were more clearly divided into male and female spheres. For the ordinary middle-class home owner, the choice depended almost entirely on personal preference.

By the 1870's this situation had become more complex. If one accepted Eastlake as an aesthetic lawgiver, and many did, then the style he advocated was not merely another alternative, it was the only *right* choice—with all the inherent moral connotations of the word. As a result, people frequently opted for a particular form of art furniture not because they necessarily preferred it to other styles, but because they felt that it had the moral sanction of some excessively re-

Oak Elizabethan-style
hall bench, c. 1840

spected aesthetic oligarch—generally quite wrongly because
trade art styles were usually little more than caricatures of
their models. This abrogation of responsibility for aesthetic
choice is one of the underlying causes of the stylistic uncer-
tainty evident in so much mid- to late Victorian furniture.

At the International Exhibition of 1862 in London,
William Burges and the firm of Morris, Marshall, Faulkner &
Co. (later William Morris & Co.) first put their furniture on
public display. Although in both cases it came under the
general heading of Gothic, Burges' and Morris & Co.'s
painted decoration was very different from the normal trade
version of the style. What really distinguishes this type of
Gothic is that it represents a genuine attempt to capture
the spirit of the Middle Ages, and it is medievalism, as we
shall see, that provides a key to the understanding of the art
furniture styles of the late 1860's to 1880's.

Similar though Burges' and Morris & Co.'s exhibits of
1862 at first appear, there is one significant difference
between them. Whereas Burges' furniture is very carefully
made, Philip Webb's designs for Morris & Co. are, by virtue
of their rougher construction, much more like the actual

work of a medieval joiner, and this quality links Morris & Co. to the Early English, or Modern English Gothic style, which was popularized by Charles Lock Eastlake in his *Hints on Household Taste,* 1868.

The historical allusions in Eastlake's interpretation of the style are even more misleading than usual because they refer not so much to outward appearance, but to the method of construction which, like medieval joinery, involved the use of pegs instead of glue. The Early English style rejected almost everything that had preceded it: curves and excessive carving because they were vulgar, structurally unsound, and involved unnecessary expense; and French polish because it prevented the furniture acquiring the patina of age. As in the best modern furniture, detail was replaced by mass, and the cabinet-maker's skill by a respect for the natural qualities of the materials used.

Bruce Talbert was held by contemporary critics to be the

The St. George cabinet, 1861. Designed by Philip Webb and painted by William Morris

supreme exponent of Early English and his sideboards
(which he considered to be the most important single item
of furniture) were universally admired. Many also are fond
of Philip Webb's massive tables.

To only link William Morris with the extremely artificial Early English style is to ignore his real historical importance. Like Pugin, Morris contrasted the age in which he
lived with the Middle Ages, and he concluded that the lack
of identification with one's work, which arises from mass
production methods, was one of the chief causes of social
unrest. The Middle Ages, on the other hand, he saw as
a socialist Utopia in which the dignity of labor was respected
and the craftsman was contented because he had the satisfaction of seeing a project through from beginning to end.
This satisfaction was, in turn, reflected in the quality of
his work.

When William Morris and his friends founded 'The Firm',
they tried to recapture this spirit, believing that they could

combine contentment for themselves with the idealistic aim of bringing art to the masses in the form of well-designed goods that were functional, beautiful and cheap. But it did not take them long to see that this was impracticable: individual designs are inevitably expensive, and Morris & Co.'s were no exception. So they began to produce furniture on two levels: the state furniture, as Morris called it, and cottage-style furniture.

If Morris & Co.'s state furniture represents the perfectionist aspect of the medievalist philosophy of the contented artist-craftsman, their cottage furniture is nearer to both the original evangelical aims of its founder members, and the theoretical basis of the Arts and Crafts Movement of the 1880's. Today, Morris' initial aim of functionalism is hardly thought of as revolutionary, but that is because we see functionalism as a virtue and simplicity as beauty. Around the 1860's and 1870's, however, functionalism was tolerated in only one room in the house, the kitchen, and beauty was still generally equated with decorative elaboration.

(*left*) Oak and box-wood sideboard by Bruce Talbert, 1867

(*right*) One of William Morris's 'Sussex' chairs

Another aspect of the all-pervading medievalism was the Japanese craze of the 1870's and 1880's. As Burges himself explained, what made Japan and North Africa so interesting was that there the medieval tradition was a living tradition. The Japanese style was necessarily restricted to the use of bamboo, decorative motifs and to a general feeling for lightness; direct copying was rare because the Japanese have less furniture than Europeans. Yet for all its artificiality, this new style was a welcome relief from the lumpiness of the popular trade baronial of the 1870's and 1880's. Of the designers influenced by Japanese art, the name of Christopher Dresser springs most readily to mind, but the best individual item must surely be E. W. Godwin's superb sideboard.

The work of top designers then, as now, was beyond the financial reach of all but a small minority, so for the mass market the trade concocted 'art furniture' which combined elements of the various stylistic innovations previously men-

Japanese-style sideboard in ebonized wood, designed by E. W. Godwin, c. 1867

Sideboard in carved oak, 1875

tioned here. The hard core of art furniture, with the exception of chairs, tended to be relatively lightly constructed in ebonized wood (until it began to be replaced by brighter woods, like satinwood, in the 1880's) usually with slender turned vertical elements. Gold was used to emphasize detail, and painted panels and turned balusters provided the main decorative element. If carving was used at all, it seldom consisted of anything more than Japanese ornamental motifs carved in boxwood. For some people all this was a little too extreme, and they remained faithful to a dark heavy baronial

23

style with flat incised pillars and Jacobean overtones, the appalling dullness of which defies description. All one can say is that it must have been designed by the same sort of person who recommended 'gray paper for the drawing room with inscriptions from the book of Job such as "Man is born unto travail as the sparks fly upwards" painted in black letters in diagonal lines' (Anon. *A Plea for Art in the Home*).

With art furniture of various types stealing the critical limelight, there is a real danger of ignoring the changes affecting the French style. In 1855 the Louis XVI style was revived at the Paris Exhibition, and by the early 1860's it was firmly established. In direct contrast to the simple decorative aids normally used by the early Victorian manufacturers (plain monochrome veneers where solid wood was not preferred in the first place, French polish, and varying amounts of ornamental carving), the Louis XVI style restored to the cabinet-maker not only the more exotic woods (in place of the stereotyped mahogany, rosewood, walnut and oak), but also such embellishments as marquetry, ormolu, porcelain plaques and buhlwork.

Closely linked with this was the so-called Adam revival in which, for the first time, the Victorians turned for inspiration to the work of English eighteenth-century cabinetmakers. The famous Wright and Mansfield cabinet exhibited in 1867 (now in the Victoria and Albert Museum) represents a key point in this development. Though basically eighteenth century in inspiration, it also incorporates porcelain plaques and other embellishments more in the French tradition. It was as if the Victorians had still not quite come to terms with the idea that beauty and simplicity were not necessarily incompatible. But within a decade numerous faithful copies (as well as a host of adaptions) of Chippendale, Hepplewhite, Sheraton and Adam designs were being produced. In the 1880's there was even a minor Queen Anne revival to match a similar revival in architecture.

The 1880's also bring us to the Arts and Crafts Movement, and much of what was already said about William Morris & Co. is equally applicable here. There is the same ideologically inspired tendency to form cooperatives of artist-craftsmen, the same emphasis on the importance of the

Painted satin-
wood chair in
revived 18th-
century style,
1880

individual member under-
standing and, ideally, carry-
ing out every process in the
production of a given article;
the same evangelistic aim of
bringing art to the masses,
and the same economically
induced failure to do so.

From a historical point of
view the Movement is ex-
tremely important because,
together with the work of
Morris & Co., it represents
the fountainhead of modern
design. Instead of being
thought of as a mere em-
ployee, the designer was
now regarded as an independent artist with a right to
self-expression (which accounts for the lack of a clearly defined Arts and Crafts
style. Finally, William Morris and the Arts and Crafts
Movement stressed the im-
portance of texture in design.

However, the influence of
the Movement on the gen-
eral public at the time was
by no means great. Apart
from its cost, the furniture
was, on the whole, too hon-
est, too individual and, by
Victorian standards, too
plain to gain a significant following outside the artistic
fringe.

Ernest Gimson's interpretation of
the traditional ladderback chair,
c. 1888

The first of the Arts and Crafts cooperatives to be established was the Century Guild, founded by A. H. Mackmurdo in 1882. This was soon followed by a number of others, the most important of which was probably C. Ashbee's Guild and School of Handicraft (1888). More radical in outlook was the Cotswold School. It was set up by Ernest Gimson and Sidney and Ernest Barnsley in Cirencester in 1893, and it included many of the former members of the short-lived Kenton & Co., among them W. R. Lethaby. The bulk of their furniture was much more in the cottage tradition, if we use Morris's distinction between cottage and state furniture, than the work of most other Arts and Crafts designers.

Until 1890, Victorian art was dominated by historicism, either directly in the form of stylistic borrowings, or indirectly as in the case of the philosophical basis of the Arts and Crafts Movement. But, as the century neared its end, and people looked forward to a new era, we see the beginnings of a corresponding shift in their attitude to art. Art

This oak desk, designed by A. H. Mackmurdo, c. 1886, had a profound influence on subsequent late Victorian furniture design.

Oak chair designed by
C. R. Mackintosh, c. 1897

Nouveau, the result of this reappraisal, was novel not only because, in theory, it rejected all links with the past, but also because, like modern design, instead of thinking of an object in terms of form and decoration, it sought to combine both these elements in one organic entity.

If we consider Art Nouveau as an international movement, we cannot fail to realize that the version of the style we see in the work of major English designers of the period is very different from that of their continental equivalents. Whereas the work of the latter is characterized by a striving after three-dimensional fluidity, English Art Nouveau restricts itself almost completely to two-dimensional planarity, a sensible decision in an age before the invention of plastics. Unlike Henri van de Velde, the Belgian designer, who vainly fought against the right angle (see his famous pedestal desk), English designers not only accepted it but, as in the case of Mackintosh's and Mackmurdo's furniture, actually made it the focal point of their designs.

Inlaid mahogany washstand, c. 1900. Perhaps made by Maples

Oak writing desk with copper hinges designed by C. F. A. Voysey in 1896

Oak chair by C. F. A. Voysey, c. 1897

In England, Art Nouveau occurred on three levels: at the extreme, the work of independent designers like A. H. Mackmurdo, C. F. A. Voysey, Baillie Scott and Charles Rennie Mackintosh; at the other, the mannerist 'Quaint' style of the trade; and somewhere in the middle, firms like J. S. Henry's and Liberty's whose value was recognized far more on the continent than in England.

Mackmurdo, Voysey, Scott and Mackintosh all produced furniture in the specifically English version of the Art Nouveau idiom but, with Voysey and Mackintosh in particular, other influences were of equal or even greater importance. Voysey, for instance, was much closer to the Arts and Crafts Movement than to Art Nouveau in both his general outlook and his use of materials. As for Mackintosh, his furniture is primarily an extension of his architecture. In each instance it was designed for a specific setting, and viewed out of context it loses much of its validity. Admittedly, this concept of the *Gesamtkunstwerk* (in which all the arts contribute to the total effect) was one of the prime aims of Art Nouveau, but perhaps with Mackintosh it was more a case of the subjugation of one form of applied art to another, than of the fusion envisaged by Art Nouveau theorists.

For the most part, however, Art Nouveau was a trade style; its exaggerated attenuation and plant-like curves, its veneers and elaborate inlays of glass and pewter, as well as of all kinds of woods, represented a reaction against the comparatively utilitarian furniture of the previous 15 years. But, as so often happens, reaction led to overcorrection, and functionalism was rejected along with utilitarianism.

Whereas for the major independent designers, functionalism was an essential ingredient of design, for the trade, effect came before anything else. Whatever the stylistic exaggerations of a chair by Scott, Voysey or Mackintosh, one can at least sit on it in safety if not always in comfort. With chairs in the 'Quaint' style there is no such guarantee because fashionable attenuation was deemed more important than structural soundness. It is interesting to speculate what the effect of such modern materials as fiberglas would have been on Art Nouveau. Would we then have had furniture as satisfying in plastic terms as Tiffany's glass?

Sofas, settees, ottomans

Around 1835 the Grecian was the most popular style for double-ended sofas. The old sub-classical rectangular shape with heavy acanthus leaf decoration on the faces of the arms was still made for more conservative clients, but the type with double-scroll ends was more common. The latter variant was often still light and simple, especially when intended for use in the hall. By 1850, however, it had become coarse and bulbous, and the acanthus leaves, which by now also decorated a large mahogany back-rail, looked more like wilting aubergines.

In spite of the immediate popularity of the style, Louis XIV sofas are rare. At their best they have the massive gilded presence of Old Venetian furniture. The basic shape was still the rectangle, but under the influence of the characteristic scroll decoration most of the right angles were rounded off.

This process of rounding-off reached its climax in the Rococo Louis XV style where the only straight line is the horizontal of the upholstered seat. The double-ended sofa in this style looks like Siamese twin tub chairs joined at the hip. In the 1840's, in common with other upholstered furniture, none of the woodwork of the back was visible, but by the 1860's all restraint had vanished. The curves were even

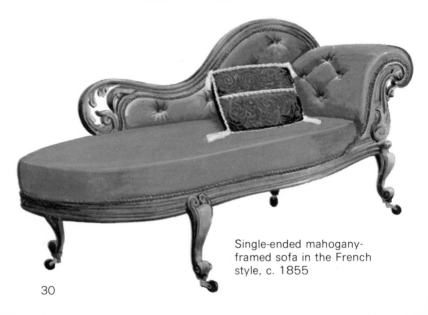

Single-ended mahogany-framed sofa in the French style, c. 1855

Three-seated chair in
carved walnut, c. 1850

more exaggerated; a third oval back-piece was often placed
between the two humps, and the whole back was decorated
with elaborate fretwork. The 1850's also saw a profusion of
peculiar multiple-seated sofas, the most typical of which was
probably the 'sociable' which usually consisted of two linked
easy chairs, either side by side or facing each other. Mahogany
and, later, walnut were the most popular woods.

Elizabethan and Gothic sofas are comparatively rare;
Gothic because of its religious associations and Elizabethan
because it was not often used for sitting rooms. But a number
of simple rectangular hall sofas, usually in oak, were made in
both these styles, particularly in the early part of the period.
The development of the single-ended sofa was similar to that
of the double-ended and requires no separate analysis.

Practically all Victorian sofas up to the 1870's are worth
buying; after that one has to be slightly more careful. The

rail-backed later version of the single-ended sofa comes in the 'good value' category. It is cheaper than its predecessors but, like other furniture of its period, it is also less attractive. Art furniture is generally unsuccessful except for the humorous interior decorator, and we have to wait until the chesterfield and the flimsy, but elegant, inlaid and painted satinwood eighteenth-century revival sofas before we have anything to compete with the early Victorian styles. The worth of the heavily button-upholstered chesterfields has already been recognized and, judging by the current trend in clothes, it is only a matter of time before late Victorian Adam revival furniture with its characteristically tapered legs becomes as popular as Art Nouveau. It already has in Italy.

The ottoman, another member of the sofa family, is also worth buying if one has enough room for free-standing furniture. Its variants range from the upholstered box with a central back to a four-segmented cake of easy chairs and sofas, with visible woodwork and either turned or cabriole legs.

(*top*) Late Victorian chesterfield

(*right*) Hepplewhite-style sofa

(*left to right*) Mahogany-framed
tub chair, c. 1850; papier-mâché
prie-dieu, c. 1850; mahogany-
framed easy chair based on the
fauteuil shape, c. 1855; mid-
Victorian armchair

Easy chairs

The most common type of early Victorian easy chair was
loosely based on the *fauteuil* (armchair) of eighteenth-century France. Usually of mahogany or walnut, it had either
turned or cabriole legs and a high rounded back with but-
ton upholstery. In some the armrests formed an integral part
of the back unit; in others the back was corseted and the arms
were merely thin padded rails. Smaller, lower versions of
the basic *fauteuil* pattern, commonly known as ladies' chairs,
were made with the crinoline in mind, so they either have
rudimentary arms or no arms at all. Unfortunately, all the
chairs in this category are expensive.

The tub-shaped chair was also popular. The upholstery craze of the 1840's made it look a little too lumpy, but later versions, with their slightly longer cabriole legs and either plain mahogany or gilded framework, are considerably more elegant. Their only drawback is that often there is nowhere to put one's elbows, so consequently they are not quite as comfortable as they might appear to be.

No such complaint can be made of the so-called library chair which came into fashion in the 1840's. Originally its back and arms formed one single unit in the shape of a horizontal horseshoe. By the mid-1870's the inevitable row of turned balusters had been worked into the design but, for once, they may have been an improvement.

Perhaps the most characteristically Victorian of all is the *prie-dieu*, a chair with a high padded back and a cross-piece at the top to act as an armrest when its owner knelt to pray. This chair is a very handsome object, and if you can find one at a reasonable price, buy it, because it is a piece with enough personality to become the focal point of a decorative scheme.

After the mid 1860's comparatively few easy chairs are worth buying. Those in the Early English style, for instance,

Horseshoe-backed chair by C. W. Trapnell, 1874, and (*right*) armchair of the post-Eastlake school

give the impression of being knocked together out of a job lot of oak planks, and their heavy rectangular leather backs and armrests do nothing to dispel the impression. Even the adjustable armchair made by Morris & Co. from about 1866 onward is inelegant compared either with early Victorian easy chairs or with his own 'Sussex' chair of the same period.

Armchairs—I hesitate to use the term easy chair because its implication of comfort may mislead—in the 'Quaint' style are often loosely based on the many different types of the traditional Windsor chair. In isolation, with their tall backs and their slats in the form of floral spears spread at the top and gathered together at the bottom, their curves and the richness of their inlaid rosewood, they are magnificent. But even more than chairs in the revived English eighteenth-century styles they demand the correct environment.

Ordinary easy chairs of the 1890's, though considerably more comfortable than those in the Early English style, are equally devoid of elegance. Many of them, with their seats almost twice as long as their backs, look like heavily upholstered daybeds for dwarfs. But there are exceptions to the rule.

Morris & Co. easy chair, 1866, and (right) heavily upholstered chair, c. 1895

Other chairs

The main distinction, particularly in the first half of the Victorian era, between dining, bedroom and drawing room chairs is one of sturdiness. The dining room versions were the most solid, next came the drawing room chairs which were 'for best' and, finally, there were the flimsier boudoir chairs, often made of stained beech and with cane seats in place of the normal upholstery.

By far the most common type of Victorian chair was the balloon-back which evolved in the 1830's and remained in fashion until the late 1860's. The typical drawing or dining room chair of 1830 had a basically rectangular back with a horizontal splat and a horizontal yoke-rail continuing beyond the uprights. But within a decade the yoke-rail had lost its overhang, its corners had been rounded, and instead of being a solid horizontal block to the vertical line of the uprights it was now a curved link between them. The loss of horizontal rectilinearity was echoed in the vertical plane by the slightly

Carved rosewood chair, c. 1835

Carved mahogany drawing room chair, c. 1855

36

Carved mahogany chair, c. 1845

corseted look given to the uprights themselves. This ungainly compromise was soon rounded off into the familiar balloon-back. The process reached its logical conclusion in the 1850's when cabriole legs replaced the straight turned front legs. Good examples of this classic Victorian shape are always worth buying, even singly. Whether in walnut, rosewood or mahogany, they are well made, elegant, comfortable and remarkably sturdy.

Second only to balloon-backs in popularity were chair in the Elizabethan style. Though called Elizabethan, the majority of them were modeled on late seventeenth-century originals. They have high backs with barley-sugar twist columns, but in place of the usual canework the Victorians often put upholstery and Berlin-work panels. Oak and mahogany are the most commonly used woods, but I have seen some in rosewood. Again, there are several variations on this theme and all of them are well worth buying.

Chair designed and made by Henry Eyles of Bath for the Great Exhibition. Its companion had a porcelain plaque with the portrait of Prince Albert.

37

Of the few ordinary chairs made in the Gothic style, the majority belong to the early part of the period. Often the Gothic ornament is extremely fanciful but there are notable exceptions, such as Pugin's magnificent carved oak armchair for Scarisbrick Hall (1840).

Historically, chairs in the Louis XIV style are extremely important because their curved scroll-decorated yoke-rail clearly influenced the development of the balloon-back. But it is difficult to be enthusiastic about them as chairs; the style was far more suitable for larger items like sofas.

Two other types of chair which are becoming increasingly popular today are a straight-backed long-legged chair designed by Sir Astley Cooper to correct children's posture,

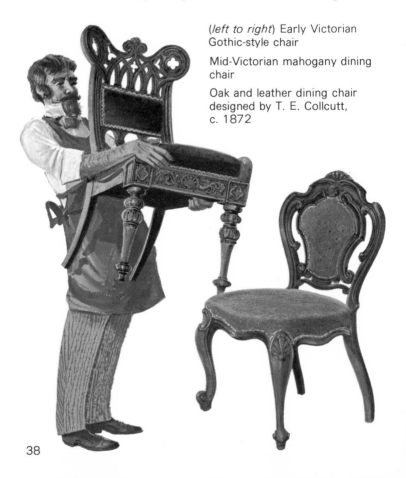

(*left to right*) Early Victorian Gothic-style chair

Mid-Victorian mahogany dining chair

Oak and leather dining chair designed by T. E. Collcutt, c. 1872 and the carved hall chair. The latter underwent little change during the period but, nevertheless, early examples are always preferable because their carving is richer and their proportions more decisive. Later versions are an unpleasant shade of tom-cat yellow and the meanness of their carving, combined with half-hearted patches of inlay, give them a somewhat stringy look that runs contrary to their essential quality of uncompromising assertiveness. The woods used range from mahogany and oak to yew.

By the late 1850's and early 1860's one can see how restive the furniture trade was becoming with current styles. Many of the chair designs registered at the Patent Office were extremely bizarre. The backs are a mass of fretwork, and the legs curve in and out as if the chair was suffering from some appalling bone disease.

Reaction, unfortunately, produced little that was worthwhile. Both Morris and Co.'s cottage-style chairs and E. W. Godwin's early designs were islands of inspiration in a morass of knobbly turning, Berlinwork and heavy rectangular backs. Even Collcutt's oak dining chair (about 1872), which represented the basic pattern for the next 20 years, is only marginally better than its trade variants. Art furniture and mid-Victorian baronial could possibly come into fashion,

(*far right*) Early Victorian oak hall chair in the Elizabethan style

but I doubt it. If I had to choose anything from the late 1860's and the 1870's I would choose either the revived Louis XV or Louis XVI style, but the closer these chairs are to their originals the more expensive they become.

The eighteenth-century revival, prompted as much by revulsion from previous excesses as by a new-found appreciation of the merits of that age, reached its height in the 1880's. The work produced in this idiom falls into three categories. First there are the direct copies which, from a design point of view, are mere sterile artifacts; then there are the adaptations, and lastly there are designs which have only superficial connections with the style on which they claim to be based. The first category one can accept because of its reflected glory, and the third because its original content far exceeds its derivative content. But the second category presents a problem because, though it may have suited contemporary tastes, later generations naturally compare original and adaptation on equal terms, and in almost all cases it is the original that comes out on top. It is the presumptuousness of these imagined improvements that I find so disturbing.

Mid-Victorian walnut dining chair   Louis XV-style walnut chair

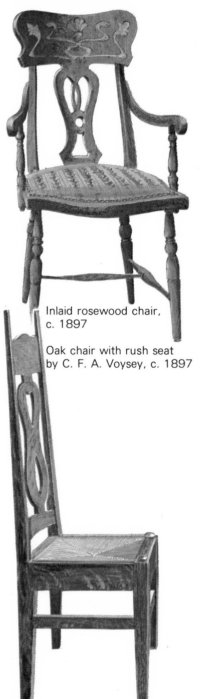

Inlaid rosewood chair, c. 1897

Oak chair with rush seat by C. F. A. Voysey, c. 1897

As I have said before, though of enormous historical importance, the work of the Arts and Crafts designers represented a minority taste. One can always idly hope to find a Gimson ladderback, but usually one has to compromise with trade interpretations of Arts and Crafts originals.

With Art Nouveau, however, the choice is wider. For those who prefer a degree of restraint, there are trade versions of designs by such people as Voysey, Mackintosh and George Walton. The most common type of chair in this category is made of oak and has a square seat. Its back is very tall and the decorative element consists either of a large number of horizontal bars between the uprights of the back or of a vertical centerpiece with fretcut heart motifs. There are many variations on this basic theme. The pure trade style, on the other hand, with its elaborately inlaid rosewood and sinuous curves based on floral shapes could hardly represent more of a contrast. But one point common to both versions is that the decoration is almost invariably concentrated on the chair back.

41

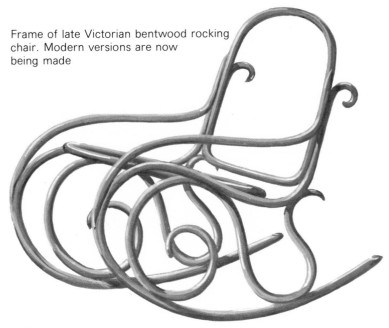

Frame of late Victorian bentwood rocking
chair. Modern versions are now
being made

Bentwood chairs, though developed by the Austrian designer Michael Thonet in the mid-nineteenth century, are one of the best examples of a really modern approach to design. They are light, cheap, durable and, especially in the case of the bentwood rocking chair, extremely comfortable and elegant. The bentwood rocking chair must surely be one of the classic designs not only of the Victorian era but of all time.

Tables

The loo table, named after the eighteenth-century card game, is a pedestal table about four feet in diameter. In the early examples, which are made of either rosewood or mahogany, the column, in the form of a truncated cone, stands on either a triangular or less frequently on a circular or rectangular base, often supported by small lion's paw feet. By the mid-1840's, the center of gravity moved upward, and the base block has been either partially or completely absorbed in the curve of the legs. By the 1860's this basic shape changed almost beyond recognition. The top is now oval and almost always inlaid, and the single pedestal has fragmented

Good-quality early
Victorian rosewood
loo table

Carved English oak
table with Worcester
porcelain plaque
designed by Henry
Eyles, 1851

into a cage of four or five smaller functional and non-functional columns. Walnut is the favored wood and, like the chairs of the same period, the tables often have decorative carving in low relief. On the more fancy examples in ebonized wood, the carving is replaced by ormolu. Yet, however fine the workmanship, I cannot make myself actually like this type of table; it is too fussy, too busy. Its predecessor, on the other hand, is very appealing and can still be bought for considerably less than a modern dining table of the same size.

Detail of mid-Victorian loo table with lavish ormolu decoration

Another type that makes an excellent dining table, particularly in a small modern apartment is the traditional rectangular drop-leaf. It is usually about three feet long and about a foot wide, but with both its leaves up it can comfortably seat eight. For those who consider the long leaves ungainly, the Victorians also made a version with half-leaves. This type makes an excellent hall or small dining table.

When it comes to occasional tables, the list is almost endless. There were

Small early Victorian tripod table

work tables, games tables, fern tables, teapoys, card tables and many others. Among the simplest is the small elegant tripod table which, like the drop-leaf table, was merely the continuation of a long-established design. The more formal early ones are made of solid mahogany, or less often, of rosewood, and are usually expensive. But cheaper, more roughly constructed, country versions in beech or oak can still be found. Sometimes these tables were inlaid with a chessboard pattern and were used as games tables. There were also very small circular tables with a triangular base, but these, though pleasant enough, are slightly unsatisfactory in shape because the tops are really too small for the height of the pedestals.

Small rectangular occasional tables are equally numerous, and it is interesting to note how little this basic shape changed right up to the 1870's. Usually the top has one support or, in later versions, two at each end, either terminating in splayed legs with a horizontal stretcher or leading on to an I-shaped base.

Early Victorian papier-mâché teapoy

Rosewood games and sewing table, c. 1850

The work table version had a hinged top revealing neat compartments for all the odds and ends required for the needlework and embroidery of which Victorian women were so fond. The underneath part usually consisted of a bag contained within the U-shaped upper sections of the supports. Mid-Victorian work tables were of a different basic pattern. They had an inlaid walnut top half in the form of an octagonal truncated cone, and stood on a pedestal with a tripod base. The teapoy was very similar in shape. They were both beginning to go out of fashion in the mid-Victorian period.

As current prices indicate, all these tables are very much in demand. My own particular favorite is the early to mid-Victorian card table. It is both attractive and functional. It can be used either as an occasional table, or, thanks to its folding top which doubles the surface area, as a small dining table which can seat four people. The amount of decoration varies with its date of manufacture and with the style in which it was made. The Grecian was certainly by far the most popular style in the early Victorian period. From about the late 1850's, though, the decorative carving, especially at the cheaper end of the range, tends to be somewhat coarse and, as in the case of the Grecian sofa of the same period which was described earlier, this often spoils a fundamentally good design.

After 1870 few occasional tables are tempting. The octagonal ones in ebonized and gilded wood with excessively heavy turned legs and turned baluster stretchers show the same dull worthiness that characterized almost all furniture of the time. Later versions with slender curved legs and a lower shelf raised coronet-like on curved members will most likely become more popular, in spite of the flimsiness of their construction, as earlier tables become more and more expensive. Low octagonal occasional tables were also made in the Moorish style throughout the late Victorian period, but they were particularly popular in the 1880's when they were widely used in smoking rooms.

The thin-legged eighteenth-century revival occasional tables, normally of satinwood with painted floral decoration, are at best a weakened version of an anemic original. And even

(*above left*) Mid-Victorian walnut-veneered work table

(*right*) Ebonized and gilt occasional table made by C. W. Trapnell, 1874

(*below left*) Early Victorian mahogany card table with strong Regency characteristics

(*right*) Typical flimsy table, c. 1890

Mahogany tea table, c. 1885. The
legs are carved to simulate bamboo.
A vast amount of genuine bamboo
furniture was made as well.

if one actually likes them, they represent a problem when it comes to furnishing a room because they contrast too much with any more vigorous style.

Quite a number of the square occasional tables of the 1870's and 1880's were loosely modeled on Godwin's Japanese-influenced prototype of 1867. But few of the adaptations are at all successful because, as Godwin himself pointed out, his design relied for its effect on the balance of all its component parts, and if anything was altered, this balance was automatically destroyed. Bamboo tables were, at this time, made in wild profusion.

So far, I have only dealt with the pedestal-type of dining table. Larger extending tables, with square or rounded ends, were made throughout the period, but they are too big for today's more modest entertaining, and used without their extension pieces they look rather clumsy. In the second half of the period, a number of heavy refectory-type tables were made. Of these, Philip Webb's are by far the best, but other post-Eastlake versions can also look good in a suitable setting.

(*above*) Mid-Victorian mahogany dining table

(*below*) Refectory-style oak table designed by Philip Webb, c. 1870. The table is actually much smaller than it looks

(*above*) Early Victorian papier-mâché music rack

(*below*) Mid-Victorian piano in burr walnut and carved and gilt music stool with Berlinwork seat

Sideboard designed for the Conservative Club (Bath Club) by Henry Whitaker, 1844

Furniture for music

No middle-class Victorian drawing room was complete without its upright piano and, for once, the supply exceeds demand. The prices today are so low that it sometimes costs more to have a piano delivered than it does to buy it. Together with the piano came the adjustable piano stool, an object of considerable charm. Heavy adjustable music stands, reminiscent of lecterns, were also popular. The floor-level music rack or Canterbury, made of papier-mâché inlaid with mother-of-pearl and painted with flowers, makes a perfect magazine rack today.

Sideboards and chiffoniers

In the early part of the reign a few Regency-style four- or six-legged slab-topped sideboards were still made for old-fashioned households or institutions like the Conservative Club, but much more usual was the rectangular pedestal type, which only differed from the basic pattern of the 1830's in that it had a higher backboard. The difference between the various styles was more a matter of ornament than of shape.

By about 1860, however, the situation had changed radi-

Cabinet of painted and ebonized mahogany by T. E. Collcutt, 1871

cally, and the French style now also differed in shape. The triple rectangular mirrors which were gradually replacing the wooden backboard in the 1840's had themselves been replaced, first by rounded mirrors and then by a single D-shaped mirror. To maintain a visual balance, a parallel development took place in the body of the sideboard to give a central cupboard with convex display shelves at either end. To complete the impression of richness, the sideboard usually had a large marble-slab top. This style remained in many trade catalogues right up to the end of the nineteenth century.

Mahogany pedestal sideboard in the Greek style, c. 1835

Sideboard of carved walnut, c. 1860. The marble top and mirror are common decorative devices in Victorian furniture

However, with the exception of the French style, the sideboard remained almost entirely in the masculine rectilinear tradition and, as a direct consequence, the basic pedestal shape recurs frequently throughout the period.

With art furniture, the high backboard, which until then had generally been purely decorative, was transformed into a series of display shelves, and the sideboards came to look more and more like a superior version of the traditional kitchen dresser. Unfortunately, it did not share its unassuming dignity. Collcutt's sideboard of 1871 with its display shelves, ebonized wood, turned supports, painted panels and floral motifs shows this style at its best. But what a poor best compared either with the massive presence of the earliest Victorian sideboards or with the simple honesty of the work of designers like W. R. Lethaby. Apart from the sideboards in various art styles, the trade in the late Victorian period concentrated its efforts on mock-Georgian and mock-Jacobean.

On the continent one of the stylistic hallmarks of Art Nouveau was the use of semi-decorative external rib-struts. In England the non-structural extensions of the uprights fulfilled the same function—which partly accounts for the comparative restraint of sideboards and other larger items of English Art Nouveau furniture. Capped uprights, stylized floral motifs or cut-out heart shapes were usually considered enough for the title of Art Nouveau. The theoretical synthesis of form and decoration was seldom attempted and wisely so.

Beautifully made Arts and Crafts oak dresser, inlaid with various woods, designed by W. R. Lethaby, 1900

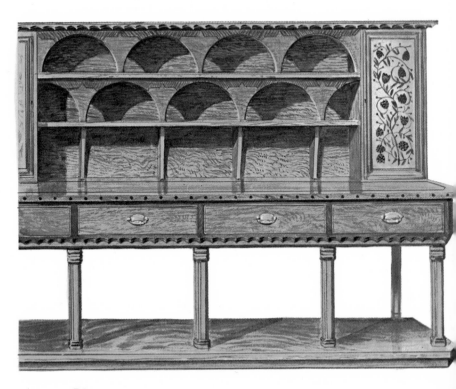

The chiffonier, which quickly became similar enough to the sideboard to virtually duplicate its function on a smaller scale, showed a parallel development. The basic pattern of the 1830's consisted of a cupboard with wire-grill doors and, above it, a backboard with a small projecting shelf. By about 1860 it had become D-shaped and marble-topped with a mirror back and convex shelves at either end.

One item of furniture which is generally thought of as uniquely Victorian but which actually dates from an earlier period is the whatnot, a series of progressively recessed free-standing shelves. The most perfect one I myself have seen was of rosewood with barley-sugar twist supporting columns. After the late 1850's the fussier corner variety became popular.

(*left*) Mid-Victorian walnut-veneered whatnot and (*right*) early Victorian chiffonier. By the 1850's to 1860's it had become a smaller version of the D-shaped sideboard.

Display cabinet in the revived
Adam style, c. 1885

Cabinets, bookcases and desks

Large free-standing bookcases conformed to the pre-Victorian pattern well into the Victorian period and, generally speaking, the Victorians preferred them to fitted shelves. Smaller bookcases, like small rectangular cabinets which as soon as they acquired glass doors were often themselves used as bookcases, showed little variation in shape throughout the period. They merely echoed current tastes in materials and styles of decoration.

To trace the development of the ordinary cupboard-type of large cabinet in any

Mid-Victorian cabinet

Mahogany dwarf
bookcase, c. 1840

Large breakfront bookcase, first half of 19th century

meaningful sense is very difficult since, in contrast to other items of furniture like the sideboard, the style did not necessarily dominate the shape. Each cabinet, therefore, has to be judged on its own merits. But, if one needs a display cabinet there is a straightforward choice between the heavy legless mid-Victorian French and the spidery Adam revival styles. The workmanship of the former, expecially where buhlwork and ormolu were used, is unsurpassed, and they provide a reasonably priced substitute for the real thing.

Besides being lovers of knick-knacks, the Victorians were also great letter writers, and so the period abounds in desks. As with everything else, it is the smaller specimens which are most valued today, and consequently the davenport is expensive. The davenport was a small lady's desk with side drawers and a sloping lid; it was made up to late Victorian times when its supremacy was challenged by the mock eighteenth-century style. Large pedestal desks were also popular, and those of each of the three main periods have their own charm.

The writing desk was also a familiar vehicle for Arts and Crafts and Art Nouveau designs. From a historical point of view the most important of these was A. H. Mackmurdo's desk (now in the William Morris Gallery, Walthamstow) of about 1886, as its characteristic capped strut soon became a leitmotiv of the English Art Nouveau style. Voysey's desk of 1896 (now in the Victoria and Albert Museum) provides a later version on the capped-strut theme.

(*left*) Early Victorian davenport, satinwood with rosewood banding and (*right*) *bonheur-du-jour*, c. 1855. Apart from adaptations, many almost perfect copies of 18th-century French pieces were produced

(*above*) Mid-Victorian desk with bamboo legs

(*center*) Small mahogany writing desk in the revived 18th-century style, c. 1880

(*below*) Late Victorian Queen Anne-style kidney-shaped walnut-veneered desk

(*above*) Large mid-Victorian gilt chimney mirror

(*below left*) Rococo-style carved and gilt firescreen with Berlin-work panel, c. 1840

(*center*) Early Victorian papier-mâché pole screen

The fireplace

In an age before television, the fireplace was the focal point of the room, and the Victorians devoted considerable energy to its decoration. The early Victorian gilt-framed mirror belongs to that very small category of under-valued objects. It adds depth and magnificence to a room and its slightly faded glass has none of the shrillness of a modern mirror. In contrast, late Victorian mantel mirrors with their pigeonhole display shelves have the same lack of taste as the sideboards to which they are all too obviously related.

Just as Victorian women were concerned about the possible ill effects of sunlight, so too they protected themselves from the heat of the fire with various types of screens. Early Victorian pole screens decorated with Berlinwork have a particular period charm—as do the later large scrapwood dividing screens that one finds either in jumble sales or chic antique shops.

Late Victorian ebonized and gilded overmantel

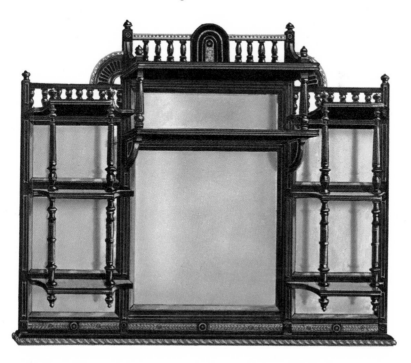

The bedroom

At the beginning of the period the heavy four-poster was the most common type of bed, but the half-tester, which had two posts, a canopy, and side curtains screening the upper end of the bed, gradually took over around the 1860's. Four-posters and half-testers are really too tall for most modern houses and any form of cutting down spoils their lines, but naturally they look marvelous in an older house with high ceilings.

In the second half of the period, the familiar brass bedstead replaced the earlier wooden one. Like chesterfields, brass bedsteads have been grossly underrated until relatively recently. Although the use of papier-mâché was generally

(*far left*) Papier-mâché half-tester bed. The papier-mâché was purely decorative; the load-bearing substructure was of iron

(*left*) Early Victorian circular marble-topped bedside cabinet

(*right*) Victorian brass bed and early Victorian washstand and mirror

restricted to smaller items like trays, tables and chairs (all of which are now very expensive), it was also occasionally used for bedsteads.

Small bedside cupboards are all worth collecting—with the inevitable exception of those in the various art styles. Particularly satisfying are the very early circular marble-topped ones. Even more attractive than early Victorian mahogany dressing tables are the originally cheaper versions in pine which look (and smell) superb when stripped of their layers of paint and varnish and polished with beeswax.

For the first two-thirds of the period the dressing table mirror consisted of a separate tray dressing glass; generally rectangular, the alternative shield-shape is also fairly common. The pattern is basically Georgian, but fatter and heavier. With the Adam revival, the mirror was incorporated into the dressing table itself. These dressing tables, like the washstands and the wardrobes that match them, are still very cheap. Their proportions are not bad, and they can look quite pleasant in any bedroom, but the workmanship already shows the beginnings of the plywood and glue tradition, with badly fitting doors and wobbly legs.

The bedroom chest of drawers provides a complete contrast to this infuriating flimsiness. The earliest versions differ from their eighteenth-century predecessors only in that they have turned legs and wooden knobs. Cheap pine chests of this type look marvelous when stripped and polished, though they do impose their own mood on their environment.

By the 1860's the chest was taller and the top one of the four drawers was often replaced by a number of small trinket drawers. Decorative pilasters, also introduced about this time, did nothing to improve the design.

The most satisfying of all is the military chest. Basically, it is a chest of drawers composed of two stout mahogany or cedar boxes, with sunken brass handles and brass-bound corners, placed on top of each other. Its absolute functionalism has made it perhaps the most popular single item of Victorian furniture, and unscrupulous dealers will adapt anything that remotely resembles it. Modern reproductions are generally no cheaper, and their wood lacks the satiny depth that only age and constant use can give.

(*left*) Late Victorian mock-Georgian mahogany dressing table
(*above*) Late Victorian mahogany chest of drawers
(*below*) Modern version of the traditional military chest

Large Victorian wardrobe

Victorian wardrobes have been much maligned—they were by no means all large and ugly. Heal's, for example, produced a simple small mahogany version almost without change from about 1840 until 1896. Even the larger ones are infinitely preferable to the shoddy anemic mock-Adam variety. It only requires a little imagination to design a bedroom, using rich heavy colors, around an enormous wardrobe of the type produced in the late 1840's. Such an item only becomes a problem if you try to pretend it is not there. The wardrobe of the 1860's, elaborately decorated with carved fruit, flowers and the apparently inevitable canine head, is more difficult to deal with, but it is certainly worth considering as an amusing alternative to the frightening expense of built-in cupboards.

Unless one already has a wardrobe with a full-length mirror on one of its doors, the cheval glass (an enormous version of the free-standing dressing table mirror) is both useful and, because of its size, still remarkably inexpensive.

The kitchen

The best way to get a good idea both of the Victorian kitchen and of the school-like orderliness of Victorian domestic life is to look through an early edition of Mrs. Beeton's *The Book of Household Management*. As the first glance will reveal, the well-appointed Victorian kitchen is an absolute paradise for the collector. Many of its contents, like the copper kettles, saucepans and jelly molds, the wooden flour barrels and rough earthenware dishes, are of great beauty, but they were not to the average Victorian, who only admired their functional qualities. I quote from Mrs. Beeton's description of French kitchens: '. . . ugly, rough earthenware pots and pans of every shape adorn, or rather do not adorn, the shelves.'

The most important item of kitchen furniture was the kitchen table which, according to Mrs. Beeton, 'should be massive, firm and strongly made.' It was. The top was left plain so that it could be scrubbed clean each day, and the rest of it was painted or varnished or both (as was every surface in the kitchen). These tables are superb—

Pine kitchen dresser

especially when offset by a stripped Victorian pine dresser.

Kitchen chairs, like so much else in the kitchen, usually represented a continuation of the eighteenth-century country tradition. There were ladderbacks, several types of Windsor chair, as well as the original models of Morris's 'Sussex' chair. Quite often there were also good eighteenth-century pieces which were considered old-fashioned and were therefore relegated either to the kitchen or the servants' room. It is by no means unheard of to find Queen Anne chests covered with layers of white paint.

As with anything else, the items to be found in Victorian kitchens fall into two categories. In the first are things like copper kettles, saucepans and jelly molds, ceramic spirits barrels and mahogany butler's trays, all of which are comparatively expensive wherever you buy them. The second category, however, is made up of objects whose prices vary enormously depending on where and in what condition you buy them. If either lack of time or a superfluity of money forces you to go to fashionable antique shops to buy stripped pine, you can pay as many dollars for a table or a dresser as you would, with luck, pennies in a junk shop.

The same holds true, to a lesser extent, of cast-iron cooking pots, china molds, brass candlesticks, brass scales, round mahogany-framed clocks of the type to be seen in every railroad waiting room, and even of beautifully carved wooden butter molds. In any case, searching is half the fun.

(*left*) Anglo-American mahogany-cased clock and (*right*) Mahogany butler's tray and stand

Windsor wheel-back chair (*left*)

Mid-Victorian slat-back chair (*right*)

Massive pine kitchen table and beech kitchen chair with rush seat

Silver

The Victorians were extremely conscious of status, and one of the most obvious ways of showing status was to own vast quantities of silver. Even if the styles became unfashionable, the value of the silver remained the same.

The best examples of purely prestige silver are the large non-functional objects like exhibition items, sporting trophies and naturalistic sculptured centerpieces made before about 1880 when their popularity declined. After the late 1840's exhibition items drew their inspiration above all from the work of Benvenuto Cellini, and sporting trophies merely exaggerated an already exaggerated tradition. But centerpieces, with their combination of heavy symbolism and absolute realism, represented a separate Victorian art form. Unfortunately, the sheer weight of silver used makes it

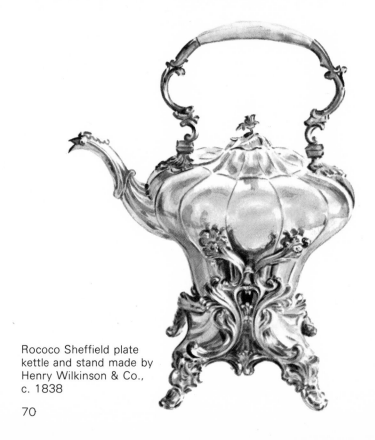

Rococo Sheffield plate kettle and stand made by Henry Wilkinson & Co., c. 1838

Elizabethan-style silver tankard, parcel-gilt, by Robert Gerrard, 1846-47. The prominent strapwork is characteristic of the style.

impossible for anyone except a millionaire to collect these fantastic creations. A collection of their titles, however, starting with *The Arab disdains all inducements of the Turkish merchant to barter for his mare and foal* is almost as good.

Testimonial silver generally occupies the next rung down the status ladder. The gift could consist of a good standard tray or teaset, but often that was felt to lack the requisite dignity, and most large silversmiths had a line in strapwork-and-cartouche decorated Elizabethan caskets.

Though these examples represent extreme cases, Victorian silver, as a whole, was plagued by the nagging suspicion that there was a direct and inevitable correlation between the number of man-hours spent on the decoration of a basic form and the value of the end product, not merely in monetary terms, but as a work of art. Manufacturers, therefore, vied with each other to provide these decorative trappings at reduced prices. This revolutionized the internal organization of the silver industry, just as it did the furniture trade. Large firms, machines and mass production techniques forced the individual craftsman out of business. The product became standardized, and even those parts of a design which were done by hand often showed the soullessness of repetitive work against which William Morris and the Arts and Crafts Movement rebelled with such vigor.

In the early part of the period, the Rococo, based on the more fanciful work of the skilled silversmiths of eighteenth-century France, was by far the most popular style. The Elizabethan took second place. The Gothic, in contrast, was rarely used for anything but ecclesiastical vessels. Classical motifs, such as acanthus leaves and husk ornament, were still used, but in debased forms. In the late 1840's and the 1850's, largely as a result of the publication of Owen Jones' *Plans, Elevations and Details of the Alhambra* (1842-45), Arabesque decoration was not uncommon.

The Elizabethan style of carving on early Victorian furniture had its equivalent in silver in the naturalistic style of the 1840's and 1850's where candlesticks became vineyards and teapots, gardens. For greater realism, instead of using castings,

(*above*) Naturalistic candlestick, 1851-52

(*top right*) Electroplated teapot, c. 1850

(*below right*) Spherical teapot, c. 1855

actual leaves were sometimes electroplated and then fixed onto whatever they were intended to decorate. Their unselfconscious exuberance makes many of the items produced in this style surprisingly attractive.

Reaction, however, was not long in coming. In an essay in the *Art Journal Catalogue* Ralph Wornum criticized English silver for its excessive ornament, with particular reference to the Rococo and naturalistic styles, and suggested a return to classical and Renaissance models. Owen Jones, too, in his *Grammar of Ornament*, 1857, advocated engraved or chased decoration in place of cast relief ornament which tended to interfere with both the shape and the function of the object it decorated.

The leaders of fashion agreed with these views but, as

in the case of furniture, the more conservative middle class still clung to restrained versions of the established styles, and until the end of the nineteenth century certain items were decorated with naturalistic ornament considered appropriate to the purpose of the object, such as fruit on fruit spoons, and vine-leaves and grapes on claret jugs.

The Greek *oenochoe* (a one-handled vase) provided the basic shape for tea and coffee pots, jugs and so on in the Greek style of the 1850's and 1860's. The Victorian version of this style differs from the eighteenth-century type in that its center of gravity was lower. To begin with, the characteristic decoration of palmettes, key-patterns and waves was remarkably restrained, but by the 1860's it was becoming less so, and the shape, particularly of the handles, was generally more stylized and angular.

The Renaissance style consisted either of copies which, though beautiful in themselves, lacked the essential slight imperfections of the original (unless an electrotype was made), or of fairly standard shapes incorporating Renaissance motifs. The

Electroplated coffee pot by Roberts & Belk of Sheffield, c. 1867

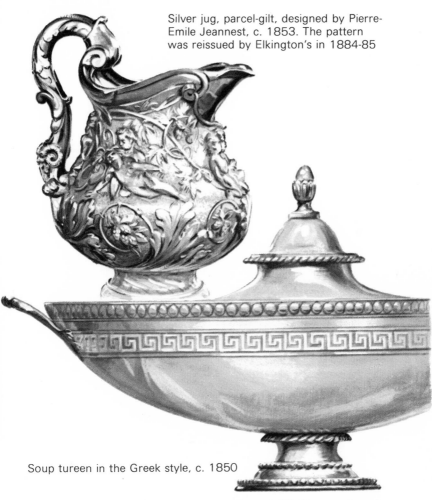

Silver jug, parcel-gilt, designed by Pierre-Emile Jeannest, c. 1853. The pattern was reissued by Elkington's in 1884-85

Soup tureen in the Greek style, c. 1850

work of Pierre-Emile Jeannest, who skillfully combined Renaissance motifs with originality, was exceptional.

In the 1870's came the Adam revival with its decorative devices of rams' heads, swags, festoons and husks. Silver continued to be made in this style until the end of the century. It was followed by a whole succession of copies and adaptations of eighteenth-century shapes, both English and French. Though more elaborately decorated and less certain in their proportions than their originals, some of them

75

Teapot in the revived Queen Anne style, c. 1885

are considered quite pleasant now and will look even better
in a hundred years time when wear and tear will have softened
their unpleasant glittery machine-made finish.

The Arts and Crafts Movement restored not only genuine
handwork but, with it, original design. The designers themselves fall into two categories: the romantics and the founders
of the modern tradition whose aesthetic code was based
on functionalism. The work of C. R. Ashbee shows the
romantics at their best. There is a real understanding both of
the natural qualities of the materials used and of the relation-
ship between them and the form chosen for a given object.

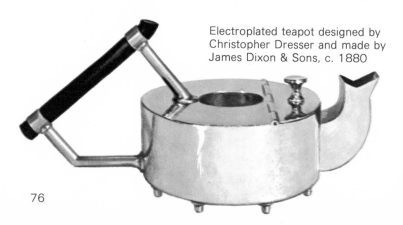

Electroplated teapot designed by
Christopher Dresser and made by
James Dixon & Sons, c. 1880

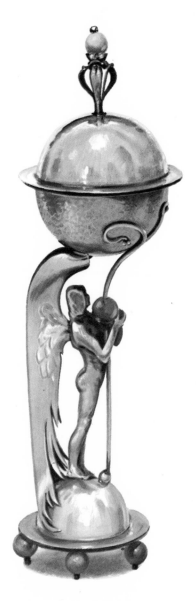

Salt cellar and cover, parcel-gilt with amber beads, designed by C. R. Ashbee, 1899–1900

Even though structural elements like rivets, instead of being invariably disguised, were sometimes incorporated into the design, the emphasis was still on the decorative. With Christopher Dresser this was no longer the case. For him, efficiency, mechanical, structural and economic, was of overriding importance, though, in practice, some elements of his designs are inevitably as arbitrary as anyone else's. The collector is helped by the fact that a number of items designed by Dresser were also made in electroplate and that Dixon's, Hulkin & Heath and Elkington's, all of whom had employed him at one time or another, produced work after his style.

Because of its ductile character, silver was, in many ways, the ideal Art Nouveau material. Certainly silver designs show a degree of inventiveness equalled only by that of textiles in the same style. And one firm, Liberty's, dominated both. For their *avant-garde* customers there were sinuous tulip-shaped silver vases with curved rib-struts forming a characteristic heart shape; for the more conservative, bowls by Bernard Cuzner which, though they incorporated Art Nouveau floral motifs, were really much closer to the work of C. R. Ashbee. There is the same feeling for purity of shape, and Cuzner even uses semi-precious stones set *en cabochon*—one of Ashbee's trademarks. For those who could not afford the 'Cymric' range of designs, Liberty's produced the 'Tudric' range of pewterware with a high silver content. Many of the designs in this range were the work of Archibald Knox. His superb jam pot (1902-03) is very similar in effect to Cuzner's covered box (1903), now in the Victoria and Albert Museum. In both cases there is perfect harmony between the lightly embossed decoration and the delicately restrained shape of the object itself. This almost classical understatement represents a complete contrast with the wild romanticism of the vase just described and shows the differences of interpretation possible within a given stylistic framework.

Silverplate
The electroplate process was patented in 1840, and the patent was bought by Elkington's whose later success was entirely based on the exploitation of this shrewd purchase. For the

(*left*) Jam pot in Liberty's 'Tudric' range by Archibald Knox, 1902–03

(*right*) Electroplated jug with engine-turned decoration, 1878–82

'Albany' soup spoon, 'fiddle thread and shell' fork, 'king's pattern' fruit knife—three common Victorian cutlery patterns

Silver cake basket, 1853–54

Victorian manufacturer, electroplating on either Britannia metal (an alloy of tin, antimony and copper), or more often on nickel silver (an alloy of nickel, copper and zinc) had many obvious advantages. The process could use the same molds as silver, so a cheaper version of a silver design could be marketed. This meant that silver plate designs remained up-to-date, while Sheffield plate designs were often years behind the current fashions because the dies cost too much to replace (this often comes as a pleasant surprise to novice collectors). If the silver wore through, the color of the nickel underneath disguised the fact; the copper of Sheffield plate did not. Nickel silver could be replated; Sheffield plate could not—hardly a disadvantage in my opinion, but for me Sheffield plate has acquired a certain aura, whereas the average early Victorian probably regarded it in as much the same light as we do nickel silver today.

Procelain

As with silver so with procelain, the Victorians borrowed many of their shapes, and a number of their styles, from the eighteenth century. The degree of actual copying varied both with the period and with the market for which the goods were intended, because accurate copies of Sèvres, Dresden and Chelsea only have a real significance for those who are familiar with the originals. Some Sèvres copies were good enough to fool even the directors of the firm making them, while in other cases the molded female masks and the painted figures clearly referred more to a Victorian than to an eighteenth-century ideal of beauty. Yet, however beautiful

Chamberlain vase,
c. 1840

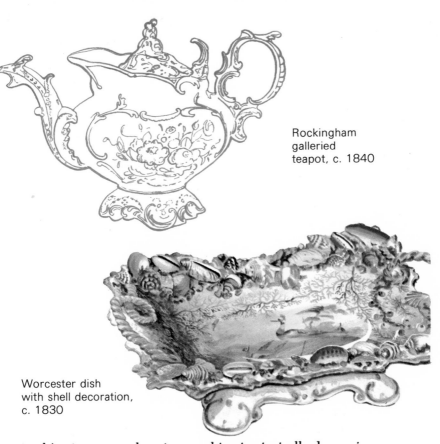

Rockingham
galleried
teapot, c. 1840

Worcester dish
with shell decoration,
c. 1830

in objective terms, there is something intrinsically depressing about actual reproductions, because they can represent artistic suicide. However, when one looks at late Victorian disasters like J. Hadley's 'Potter' vase whose only possible merit is originality, one wonders if the copyists were not right.

The revived Rococo dominated the early part of the period. Vases and other similar objects in this style are characterized by ogee curves, elaborate molding and applied irregular bouquets of flowers and, less often, fruit. Painted decoration, however, is necessarily restricted by a lack of flat surfaces. With domestic ware the problem is less acute, and slightly stylized flowers, fruit, topographical scenes and people abound. The edges of plates are often pierced or molded, and everything is richly colored and gilded.

By the 1850's Sèvres was king. Copies and adaptations were, made by most of the more important manufacturers, and a large proportion of the better porcelain was decorated in the Sèvres style.

Every action has a reaction, and the stylization of Sèvres decorative painting was followed, in turn, by a naturalistic movement which lasted until the mid-1870's. Outstanding in this field were J. Randall's paintings of birds and C. F. Hurten's flower subjects.

The Greek and Renaissance styles, which exerted such an influence on silver, also began to affect porcelain design around 1850. The Renaissance style included a number of Cellini-type ewers and the Royal Worcester 'Ivory' body nefs of the 1880's, as well as Thomas Bott's 'Limoges' style of painted decoration.

Until the mid-1860's, decoration consisted mainly of painting and gilding, but then potters became interested in the treatment of the actual surface itself. Royal Worcester produced their 'jeweled ware', their Japa-

Copeland vase and cover decorated in the Sèvres style, c. 1850

nese-style vases, their fantastic pierced ware (originated by Chamberlains in 1845), and several firms, though Minton's were the specialists, used the incredibly difficult *pâte-sur-pâte* technique.

Perhaps as a direct consequence of the growing interest in texture the quality of painting began to decline. The powerful disciplined realism of J. Randall was replaced by the mawkishly sentimental bird paintings of Desiré Leroy, and C. F. Hürten's superb flowers by rather badly drawn orchids. Landscapes, particularly in the last decade of the century, tended to be of the misty morning variety. Figure subjects showed a wider range. There were the pseudo-classical cupids of L. Besche, the insipid *fin-de-siècle* ladies in Greek costume and occasional female figures of fashion-plate realism by S. Alcock and others.

Coalport plate painted by William Cook, c. 1850

In the 1840's Coalport produced the much admired floral-encrusted porcelain known as 'Coalbrookdale'. Their copies of Sevres (William Rose developed the immensely successful 'Rose Pompadour' tint which, for a while, was quite wrongly known as 'Rose du Barry') and Chelsea are excellent, but their later jeweled ware, for all its technical brilliance, does not appeal to the modern collector.

The main Coalport ceramic artists included W. Cook (who painted fruit and flowers in the style of Sèvres); J. Rouse (Sèvres figure subjects); J. Randall (birds in the Sèvres manner and, later, in his own realistic style); R. F. Abraham (figure subjects) and J. Aston (flowers).

Copelands produced porcelain in a variety of styles and for a variety of purposes —all of a very high standard. However, they are noted above all for their development of the parian body and for the quality of their flower painting. Their chief artists were: R. F. Abraham, L. Besche and S. Alcock (figure subjects); D. Evans and his successor C. F. Hürten (flowers); D. Lucas, Jr. and W. Yale (scenes).

(*above*) Copeland ewer, painted for the 1851 Exhibition

(*below*) Copeland vase painted with flowers and gilt by C. F. Hürten, c. 1870

(*left*) Derby plaque painted by John Haslem, c. 1830–40

(*right*) Derby cup and saucer in 'Japan' style, 1810–30

The original Crown Derby factory closed in 1848, but Stevenson & Hancock produced a number of unglazed figures from eighteenth-century Derby molds. In 1876 the Crown Derby factory was revived, and after 1890 it was known as Royal Crown Derby in acknowledgement of royal patronage. Apart from the familiar blue and red gilded 'Japan' pattern (derived from Japanese brocade designs), many adaptations of eighteenth-century Derby designs were produced—as well as the inevitable Sèvres. The major Derby ceramic artists were: J. Haslem (figure subjects in the Dresden and Sèvres styles); D. Lucas, Sr. (landscapes); T. Steele (fruit and flowers); D. Leroy (birds and flowers); J. Rouse, Sr. (all subjects) and G. Cocker (figure models).

(*left*) Minton vase painted in the Sèvres style for the 1851 Exhibition

(*right*) Minton vase with pâte-sur-pâte panels and decorated with cupids, c. 1898

Minton's combined a very wide range of activities with supreme quality; they always used the best materials and employed the best artists available. They were particularly adept at reproducing old Sèvres colors, and their 'acid gold' process, which gave a relief pattern in gold, was also extremely pleasant if not overdone. Their most dramatic achievement, however, was M. L. Solon's mastery of the supremely difficult *pâte-sur-pâte* technique. This process involved the gradual building up of a workable surface by means of thin slip washes. When a sufficient depth had been achieved, the design was carved out in much the same way as a cameo. A single vase could take years to finish—and be very costly, so examples of Solon's work are of particular interest for the rich specialist.

The list of other ceramic artists working for Minton's is so long that a selection must be more arbitrary than ever. Among the most important were: figure subjects: C. Henk (mainly after the manner of Watteau), T. Allen (Sèvres style), A. Boullemier, R. Coleman, H. W. Foster (mainly portraits), A. Turner; animals: J. E. Dean, A. H. Wright, D. Leroy (birds and also flowers); flowers: R. Pilsbury, J. Smith (particularly roses). Other well-known artists like W. Mussill, E. Rischgitz, and T. Kirkby mainly decorated earthenware.

Kerr and Binns was formed in 1852 out of what was left of the Chamberlain Company. When W. H. Kerr retired in 1862, the Company became the Worcester Royal Porcelain Company. The Grainger Company remained separate until it was incorporated into the Royal Worcester Company in 1889, but even then it kept its own identity until its factory was closed in 1902. Its output, however, tended to echo the styles of its more successful rival.

(*left*) Worcester plate, 1862–71
(*center*) Minton cup and saucer, c. 1875
(*right*) Minton plate, c. 1850

Royal Worcester 'Japanese' vase, c. 1870, and poor-quality
vase, c. 1900

The *Midsummer Night's Dream* dessert service, with its
parian supports in the form of figures of characters from the
play, established the reputation of Kerr and Binns, and
Thomas Bott's Limoges-style painting, so much admired by
the Royal Pair, greatly strengthened the firm's position. In
the late Victorian period a number of styles were produced,
the virtuosity of which is admirable even if the results are
not always entirely to present-day taste. The Persian-style
vases and the Renaissance nefs are unquestionably beautiful; Royal Worcester jeweled ware and James Hadley's
Japanese-style vases are a matter of opinion, but his 'Potter'
vase can only be described as hideous. George Owen's
intricate 'reticulated' ware, yet another Royal Worcester
speciality, belongs to the Solon tradition, where the beauty
of an object was still measured in terms of the amount of
man-hours put into the making of it. Today we might consider this direct purchase of another man's life macabre.

The various Worcester companies also produced more
mundane items which echoed the styles of the day, but the
importance of these was eclipsed by the comparatively
exotic styles mentioned above.

Staffordshire pastille burner, c. 1830, and Stevenson & Hancock figure

Nor should the work of other less well-known firms be ignored. Belleek produced beautiful wares, often with marine decorative themes which, perhaps because the factory was in Ireland, are more in the eighteenth-century style than the work of almost any other Victorian pottery. Davenport also produced porcelain of great charm. Their 'Japan' pattern has often been compared with the Derby original. Moore Brothers' *flambé* vases, too, are delightful, though understandably expensive due to the technical difficulties of the glazing.

Porcelain figures are surprisingly rare in the Victorian period. Minton's produced some in the late 1830's and the 1840's; around 1845 Copeland and Garret made some very pleasant animal figures (the recumbent greyhounds are particularly attractive) and, two decades later, Stevenson and Hancock, as already noted, used eighteenth-century Derby molds for their unglazed figures. But these are exceptions to the general rule of parian, which was prized not so much because it provided an alternative body, but because it resembled marble and could therefore be used for the very Victorian purpose of bringing art to the people.

With the aid of Benjamin Cheverton's reducing machine and the sponsorship of organizations like the Art Union of London, the work of contemporary sculptors could, and often did, appear on every mantelpiece.

But the use of this new body was not restricted to miniature sculpture; it was also used, more humbly, as a basic raw material for things like mugs with high relief ornament and, more imposingly, as the decorative element in prestige pieces like the Kerr and Binns' 'Shakespeare' dessert service. Though Copeland's probably discovered the parian body, and any number of companies produced parian figures, it was the consistently high quality of the Minton products that came to dominate the market. Over the years millions of parian figures must have been made, and as they are only just beginning to return to fashion, there is still a chance of finding good examples at reasonable prices.

Minton parian figure of Mercury, c. 1850

Pottery

Victorian pottery represented a living tradition and as such has all the strength and vitality so evidently absent from the bulk of the more historically oriented porcelain of the period. The range of items manufactured was enormous but, generally speaking, everything falls into one of three broad categories: the folk art tradition, commercial mass produced and art pottery.

The first category is dominated by the flatback figure which, about the middle of the century, replaced earlier pottery figures more carefully modeled in the round. The flatback was the 'flight of plaster ducks' of its day. It was purely decorative and cheap enough for absolutely anyone to buy. It was so cheap not only because of the simplicity of its design and manufacture, but also because it was often produced by child labor. It has been calculated that a child of

Staffordshire flatback of a Highland figure

nine working a seventy hour week was expected to produce some 145,000 of these figures for the princely wage of five guineas a year.

The decoration is naturally fairly bold and simple. The only underglaze colors widely used were cobalt blue and, less frequently, black. Other colors were less likely to stand up to firing and were therefore applied in the form of overglaze enamels. Later figures have hardly any decoration at all and are generally more insipid. By the 1870's the heyday of the flatback was past, though they were still made until the outbreak of World War I. In most cases the subjects were untitled, but in view of the sheer volume of output, portrait figures (Garibaldi and the Royal Family were favorite subjects, though Thomas Balston has catalogued nearly 200 others) are also fairly common.

In much the same tradition come the fairing, cruder earthenware 'cottage' (so called from their shape) pastille

A less usual variant of the familiar 'comforter' mantelpiece ornament

Elbogen china fairing with the inscription 'The last in bed to put out the light'. Made in Germany

burners and the Maltese terrier and King Charles spaniel cross comforters. Fairings, as the name implies, came from fairs—like today's plaster Alsatians. Pastille burners lost their fumigatory function with improvements in sanitation, and from about the mid-1840's were used simply as ornaments. Comforters were occasionally used as door porters, but their main function was decorative.

More carefully modeled figures of various breeds of dog were also made throughout the period. Staffordshire produced the bulk of these dogs, although it was a common theme for a number of Victorian potteries. Among the most attractive of these are the 'Jackfield' (black-glazed earthenware with light gilt decoration) greyhounds.

Toby jugs copied from old models, cow jugs and fox-mask stirrup cups are all equally worthy of the collector's attention. But, even greater than the market for these was the market for gift, joke, and commemorative wares.

Staffordshire greyhound in black-glazed red earthenware decorated with gilding, c. 1830

Commemorative mug inscribed 'Remember me'

(*left*) Stoneware puzzle jug,
c. 1825

(*below*) Flower-painted jug made
in Bristol, 1853

Thistle-shaped loving cups continued to be produced in the early part of the Victorian period, though the two-handled mug shape is more common. They were decorated with a variety of scenes and inscriptions. Souvenir mugs with messages such as 'A Present from the Isle of Wight' or quite simply 'Remember Me' were made throughout the period, but the earlier ones have a pleasing unselfconsciousness often absent from later examples. Again, very much in the folk tradition were the frog mugs, in which a realistically modeled frog peered up at the drinker as he finished his drink. Puzzle jugs, with multiple spouts and hidden holes, guaranteed to drench the unwary user, were another favorite form of practical joke. These trick jugs showing an aspect of the English sense of humor dated back to the Middle Ages.

Commemorative jugs, on the other hand, were more dignified. The most beautiful one I have ever seen is in the Manx Museum in Douglas. It was made to commemorate the opening of the Laxey wheel (then, if not now, said to be the

The Laxey commemorative jug, 1854

Sunderland earthenware plaque with pink and copper lusters. The inscription is typical.

biggest wheel in the world), and presented to the captain of Laxey Mines. Though any number of potteries produced wares of the kinds mentioned above, those made in Sunderland up to mid-Victorian times with their characteristic combination of black transfer printing and pink luster are, in the opinion of many collectors, the most satisfying. The most popular decorative subjects were the Wearmouth bridge; nautical scenes, often with accompanying sentimental verses; and religious mottoes like 'Thou God Seest Me'. The latter were usually printed on plaques.

Most of the items I have mentioned so far have a direct and often naive beauty which, by virtue of its contrast with our own age, particularly appeals to collectors. This has inevitably forced prices up, and an object which was originally given as a fairground prize now changes hands for several pounds. But even if one cannot afford to build up a collection of Sunderland ware, there are other less expensive things to collect, particularly in the field of mass-produced domestic wares.

Charles Meigh's mug, 1847

(*below*) Color-printed plate by
F. & R. Pratt of Fenton, c. 1850

(*right*) Blue and white transfer-
printed meat dish, 1830–40

The ornamental relief decorated jug, for instance, represents folk art at a more
reasonable price. Admittedly,
the best examples are quite
expensive, but if one is
patient, they are the sort of
things that can turn up in
thrift shops at a price that
only reflects their functional
value. They generally have a
white body, glazed inside and
lightly outside. The earlier
ones are pear-shaped and
have a foot; later ones (made
after about 1850) tend to dis-
pense with the foot and are
increasingly tankard-shaped.
The decorative themes range
from genre subjects to *amor-
ini* (little cupids), from stags
to flowers and fruit, but even
those with figure motifs
usually had vegetation of
some kind as well (Wedg-
wood jasperware jugs of the
1850's show an equal fond-
ness for floral decoration).
In the late 1870's more restrained forms, either decorated with simple patterns in
low relief or with Japanese-
style bamboo and blossom
motifs, began to replace the
earlier flamboyance.

But for me the most satis-
factory item in this general
category is not a jug at all,
but a mug designed by
Charles Meigh in 1847 with

a relief pattern of dancing figures based on Poussin's *Bacchanalian Dance.*

Underglaze transfer-printed table services, however, provide the richest hunting ground for the collector because millions of pieces in thousands of patterns must have been produced. At first everything was decorated in blue because that was the only color that could withstand the heat needed to fuse the covering glaze; but, by about 1830, other colors were also used, though blue remained by far the most common.

Immediately before our period, topographical subjects were extremely popular. These included many American scenes, because right up to late Victorian times America remained one of the main markets for blue and white ware.

By about 1840, however, idealized romantic scenes, often with leaf and scroll work borders, were beginning to take the lead. Rustic scenes came a little later. Elaborate floral decoration was another popular motif. By the 1860's scenic subjects were beginning to go out of fashion. They were replaced either by flowers or, in the 1870's and 1880's, by comparatively dull Japanese motifs, though the famous Willow Pattern always remained in production.

Mason's 'Ironstone'
'Japan' pattern jug

Wedgwood Tazza (dish) painted
with a scene of women bathing
in a woodland stream by Emile
Lessore, 1861

Multicolor printing on pottery dates from the late 1840's.
The process itself was discovered at the firm of F. & R. Pratt,
one of whose specialities was the manufacture of pot lids.
Originally these decorated lids were made for the jars of
bears' grease pomade with which early Victorian gentlemen
smeared their hair (apparently some chic barber's shops even
had bears which they fattened up and sold 'on the hoof', so
that the client could judge the quality of his grease for himself). Later, lids of this type were used for paste pots.
The same technique was also used to decorate dinner services. The Americans and the continentals were very good
customers.

Of the many porcelain substitutes, Mason's Ironstone China
(patented in 1813) is the best known, and good examples of
their Imari pattern are well worth looking for. But by about
1860 the pattern was becoming rather tight and coarse.

As far as the Victorians were concerned, the common earthenware cooking pot came right at the bottom of any list, but one only has to look in a modern shop specializing in cooking utensils to see how opinions have changed. Apart from the ordinary plain examples, one sometimes comes across dishes decorated with beautiful molded designs (the best were made by Wedgwood in fine stoneware). These can cost less than the modern revivals of the same style.

The same vigorous quality can be seen in certain examples of early and mid-Victorian art pottery, particularly in the terra-cotta vases with relief decoration like the one made by Wills Brothers for the Exhibition of 1862. Terra-cotta was also widely used for garden figures and vases, and for architectural moldings. Many Victorian houses from the 1860's onward have terra-cotta fruit and flower plaques set into the brickwork. In the mid-Victorian period potteries like Watcombes and the Torquay Terra-cotta Company used this medium as a body for glazed and gilded vases and other decorative objects. Terra-cotta was also used for the so-called Etruscan ware of the 1850's and 1860's, based on Greek red-figure ware of the 5th century B.C.

Typical Victorian earthenware cooking pot

Terra-cotta vase with a relief of Diana and Actaeon made by Wills Brothers, London, 1858

Majolica, Palissy ware and the style known as Henri II, in contrast, were inspired by the work of Italian and French potters of the Renaissance. Minton's was particularly famous for these types of wares. Henri II took two forms: with or without inlaid decoration. The latter was easier to produce and considerably more attractive. The former involved making a decorative pattern of inlaid clays and, certainly to start with, the results were very expensive.

The Majolica-Palissy group of wares always presents a problem because so many different styles are covered by these titles. At its simplest, majolica referred to a green-glazed ware with a relief pattern — usually of leaves. Then at a more sophisticated level, there were plates and vases which approximated to true majolica in that they used Renaissance subjects and Renaissance arabesques but, unlike the original, the painting was seldom done on the raw glaze.

(*left*) Minton's Henri II-style ewer, 1862. The decoration is of inlaid clays
(*right*) Green-glazed majolica dish, probably Wedgwood, c. 1860

Doulton salt-glazed flask of
Prince Albert

Minton's version of the 'Hop'
jug, c. 1858. This was a copy in
Palissy ware of the original jug

Finally, there was Palissy ware which, though it originally referred to pottery in the manner of Bernard Palissy, came to mean anything with colored glazes and relief decoration. Minton's famous majolica chestnut dish of 1855, for example, is quite often described as Palissy ware.

Without Henry Doulton as head of Doultons of Lambeth, this pleasant historicism might have continued for much longer than it did. But in 1871 and 1872 he exhibited salt-glazed stoneware art pottery. We are now used to the crudeness of modern pottery and this hardly seems revolutionary to us, but the Victorians had reserved this medium for cooking pots, ginger beer bottles or, at its most ornamental, roughly modeled flasks (though the fashion for these had declined since the late 1820's and early 1830's). The experiment proved a great success among the aesthetes who were tired of historicism and of the Victorian potters' habit of trying to pretend one material was another.

Incised and painted Doulton stoneware jug decorated by A. B. Barlow, 1874. The applied beading is characteristic

One of Wallace Martin's grotesque birds, 1903

The actual Doulton pots themselves with their beading and incised decoration and their bias toward not very pleasant shades of brown and blue (again imposed by technical considerations) have a greater historical interest than aesthetic appeal. The opposite, however, is true of some of the other Doulton products like faience and the white-bodied Carrara ware.

The work of the Martin brothers represents another step toward the modern concept of the studio potter because, unlike other potteries of the time in which the designer was not involved in the technical processes of manufacture, the brothers between them carried out all the different stages of work. Their grotesque birds and 'face' jugs, with their harsh browns, greens and yellows, are instantly recognizable, but in their middle and late period they also produced more restrained work. The globular vases with incised floral motifs

Exquisite luster-painted
vase by William De Morgan,
1888–98

are particularly attractive and far more acceptable.

If it is beauty alone that interests us, we must turn to the work of William Morris's friend William De Morgan, potter and later novelist. His pottery has a perfection of shape and color which is not to be equaled by other Victorian potters. The covered luster-painted vase (now in the Victoria and Albert Museum) he is shown holding in a painting by his wife, Evelyn, is my own personal favorite Victorian pot. And, what is more, De Morgan's Persian colors (turquoise, green and blue), which he used mainly, but not exclusively, to decorate tiles, are just as attractive as his luster colors!

Walter Crane, another friend of Morris's, also designed quite pleasant luster-decorated pots, but for the most part, late Victorian art pottery, even the work of people as talented as Christopher Dresser, comes as an anticlimax after that of William De Morgan.

Glass

At the beginning of the Victorian period the quality glass industry was in a precarious position because most of its eggs were in one basket: the production of plain mitercut lead crystal, in the manufacture of which England had become the acknowledged leader. This lack of diversification and the implied unwillingness to experiment with new techniques, a state so uncharacteristic of Victorian applied art in general, was not due to indifference or complacency on the part of the manufacturers. It was the direct result of the longstanding and heavy excise levied on glass (10½d per pound of materials used in 1822). When the Glass Excise Act was finally repealed in 1845, the industry set to work to catch up the lead the Bohemians had established in the use of colored glass. Ironically, it had been the quality of English cut crystal that had originally forced others to turn their attentions to colored glass.

The growing use of steam-driven cutting wheels combined with the reduction in the cost of manufacture of glass led to a temporary boom in cut glass. It was temporary because even before the vogue had reached its height, cut glass was already becoming unfashionable among the leaders of taste. Admittedly, cut crystal, symbolized by Follet Osler's four ton, 27-foot high fountain, represented one of the highlights of the Great Exhibition, but its rapid decline after 1851

Cut glass scent bottle, c. 1850

would indicate that the admiration was possibly more for the technical virtuosity of the exhibits than for the fashion they represented. Ruskin's condemnation of cut glass in *Stones of Venice*, therefore, was a *coup de grâce* rather than a *coup de tonnerre*.

Much more important were Ruskin's views on Venetian glass, views which through the intermediary of William Morris and his followers, were to affect profoundly the future of English glass design. As W. A. Thorpe puts it in his *English Glass:* 'The two highbrow ideas were: first, that glass is made soft and should look soft, not hard like natural crystal; and second, that when glass is blown, you must get your design out of inflational play.'

Particularly in the early Victorian period the fortunes of colored, cut, engraved and pressed glass were closely linked. In the early 1840's the choice for the consumer was effectively between expensive cut glass on the one hand and either pressed or cheap colored glass in the 'Nailsea' tradition on the other. The last was cheap because, usually, though not always, it was made of unrefined bottle glass which carried a lower excise. The beautiful elaborate 'Nailsea' flasks, pipes and walking sticks are avidly collected and therefore expensive, but the simpler opaque or clear glass rolling pins, often with a sentimental message in gilt, are more reasonably priced.

Ruby glass pipe made at
Boulton's of Warrington, c. 1840

One glass from a set said to have
been designed by Philip Webb
for William Morris, 1859

Typical Victorian pub glass and custard glass

Soon the remarkably accurate pressed glass imitations of fashionable cut glass began to threaten the market for 'Nailsea' ware, so when the excise was lifted, many of the manufacturers regarded it as a heaven-sent opportunity to switch to the middle-class market, and began to produce those clear-colored wine glasses, decanters and jugs so much admired today. Ruby, green, and a yellowish tint known as vaseline were the most popular colors, but many others were also used. The shapes, too, are generally much simpler than those of more fashionable wares because, quite apart from the questions of cost and traditional conservativism, the whole middle-class way of life demanded a greater degree of functionalism than that of the rich.

The same feeling of rightness is also one of the most pleasing characteristics of Victorian trade glass best seen in solid heavy pub glasses, blown sweet jars with ground mushroom tops and, at a higher level, in the beautiful decorative chemists bottles.

With pressed glass one has to be a little more selective. The eighteenth-century derivative styles are generally better designed than other more extravagant pieces, yet the latter are worth buying for their period flavor. A style similar to the American 'lacy' style (involving the use of raised dots),

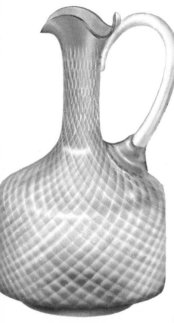

Decanter in pinkish glass known as cranberry

Small glass used in pubs

(*right*) Chemist's bottle with gilt label and cut glass stopper

(*far right*) Commemoration dish

Pressed glass tumbler

Blue and white
cased vase, c. 1850

which was fashionable in the 1870's and 1880's is often highly valued, but I myself prefer either the early large Gothic-style goblets or the slightly later simple tankard-shaped souvenir mugs, often with molded leaf decoration. Some of the colored pressed glass is also very pleasant, though with the opaque varieties in particular one has to be on one's guard for modern imitations. In fact, the choice is endless, and in the last analysis everything depends on whether one wants good design, sentiment or simple curiosity value, as in the case of the purple and white conglomerations known as 'slag' or 'end of day' glass.

Though some superior colored glass was made before 1845, in spite of the extra tax of a penny per pound, the amount was negligible compared with what was being produced at the time of the Great Exhibition. Clear glass was made in any number of colors, and opaline glass, often in the form of vases, was becoming increasingly popular. These sometimes had relief ornament of reptiles or leaves in a contrasting color. Other popular forms of decoration were

Cut and gilt opaline vase made by W. H. B. and J. Richardson in the early 1850's

straightforward painting, as in the French equivalent, and transfer printing. Plain clear glass was also painted.

It is the cased glass that really represents the high fashion of the day. Anything between two and five layers of glass were used, and the design was often loaded with additional forms of embellishment like enamel painting, gilding, cutting or engraving. Some of the more exotic versions even had a layer of silver trapped between two layers of glass! The most common, however, had clear blue or red over opaque white with an inner layer of clear glass. The cased vases dating from this period are of superb workmanship, but this is often outweighed by the strangeness of their shape and for this reason the drinking glasses are generally preferable.

Cased glass was sometimes used for lusters (high-stemmed vases or candlesticks with cut crystal pendants), but good examples of these are expensive. Simpler ones with opaque clear-colored or plain glass bodies are more common and less expensive but by no means cheap. They all look marvelous in candlelight.

The late 1840's saw the introduction into England of the *millefiori* process. The Stourbridge versions are expensive; the Clichy ones are prohibitive. Other paperweights worth looking out for are Apsley Pellatt's 'crystallo-ceramics' in which white ceramic busts are encased in crystal glass. Less pleasing, though still widely collected, are the floral paperweights with their slightly garish molded glass flowers. More functional, but cheap enough to collect in mass, are the paperweights consisting simply of a heavy clear glass blank with a print or photograph attached underneath.

As cutting began to go out of fashion as a means of decorating plain glass (to a large extent because pressed glass imitations were destroying its formerly selective appeal), engraving, and later acid etching, were frequently used instead. Both these processes had been used sparingly since the 1830's, but the mid-Victorian period was their heyday. In the 1870's another engraving process, the so-called rock-

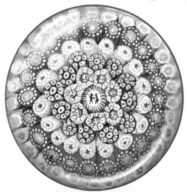

Millefiori paperweight

Cut glass bowl decorated by E. Hammond for Stevens & Williams of Brierley Hill, Stourbridge, c. 1895

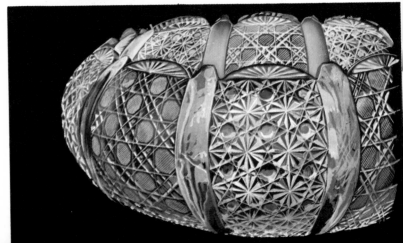

Engraved goblet showing the
Scott memorial in Edinburgh; the
hollow knop contains a coin of
1870

Cameo vase designed by
T. Woodall and worked by
J. T. Fereday, 1884

crystal technique, which involved deep cutting followed by
careful polishing of the cut edges to give an effect of ice-
cold perfection, caught the public imagination.

This, in turn, was followed by intaglio and cameo glass,
two processes generally linked with the name of John
Northwood of Stevens and Williams. Cameo glass was the
glass equivalent of *pâte-sur-pâte,* but much more difficult.

By the 1880's fashion had gone full circle and the late
Victorian cut glass revival produced work of even greater
precision, if that is possible to imagine, than the cut glass
boom of the late 1840's and the 1850's.

Small individual spirit decanter;
early 19th century

When it comes to analyzing early Victorian styles, the easiest way was to do it is to trace the changing shape of the decanter. The Regency barrel shape with its mushroom top and horizontal cutting was replaced by a longer-necked style with an onion-shaped stopper. This was followed by a version with gently sloping shoulders and a straight-sided lower half. The cutting echoed the vertical tendency of the shape itself, and deep fluting and Gothic arches were popular devices of the late 1830's and 1840's.

The Rococo style was represented by the spherical long-necked decanter, and the Greek style by the footed ovoid shape, the first examples of which appeared at much the same time as the Greek style in pottery. (Some were, in fact, painted to look like pottery.) By the 1870's this was the most common style for decanters. The Renaissance style, in contrast, generally meant little more than having Renaissance arabesques or a Renaissance subject engraved on the article in question. (Claret jugs represented the only real exception to this rule because their silver spouts, lids and handles could be molded like a Cellini ewer.)

The early Victorian version of the Venetian style always causes difficulty because, though a number of Venetian characteristics like frosting and convolution were used, little attempt was made to capture the true spirit of Venetian glass. One possible reason is that few manufacturers at that time had actually seen Venetian glass.

The development of the drinking glass is much harder to summarize but, in general terms, glasses, like decanters, became less solid. Again, as in the decanter, the cutting first took on a vertical bias, and then gradually disappeared altogether (that is, from items produced for the fashion conscious), to be replaced either by engraving on the bowl or, in the mid- and late Victorian periods, by the use of decorative techniques carried out while the glass was still plastic. With the eighteenth-century revival, elaborate cutting over the whole surface of the bowl came into fashion.

Engraved goblet of Sunderland Bridge and Exchange, c. 1825

Champagne glass, George Bacchus & Sons, Birmingham, c. 1850

(*above*) Venetian-style
green bowl made by James
Powell & Sons in 1876

(*center*) 'Burmese' glass vase by
Thomas Webb & Sons of Stourbridge, c. 1890

(*below*) Satin glass bowl with
trapped air and applied decoration
made by Stevens & Williams of
Brierley Hill, Stourbridge, c. 1885

This is only a rough guide; there was always a conservative market which ignored the pendulum of fashion and bought solid and sensible glass.

In 1859 William Morris commissioned Philip Webb to design a set of glasses which are usually taken to represent the link between Ruskin and modern glass design. The bulk of the more fashionable wares of the mid-Victorian period, however, were produced by manufacturers who took Ruskin's praise of Venetian glass more literally, and began to produce glass in the Venetian style; for glass in the Venetian spirit we have to wait for Powell. As with other Victorian styles, this could mean anything from the production of near copies to hack fantasies where the only similarity to their alleged models was the use of one or more typical Venetian decorative devices like trailing, threading, ribbing, twisting or beading. Yet even the most conscientious copyists could never be entirely successful because the Venetian soda-lime glass was far less clear than the English lead crystal, and so however plausible the shape and decoration, the quality of the medium itself was different.

Before criticizing the ultimate exaggeration of the style in the mid- to late Victorian center pieces, looking for all the world like a confectioner's dream, we would be wise to look at a genuine seventeeth-century centerpiece. The overall effect is much the same. Some of the drinking glasses, however, have a curiously pleasing quality of flamboyance and daring combined with fragility that is such a welcome relief from the functionalism of so much of today's glass. If the style of today's clothes is anything to judge by, we are due for a wholesale romantic revival, so we ought to buy these glasses while we can still afford them.

Late Victorian glass, more than any of the other applied arts of the period, was marked by the breathless pursuit of novelty for its own sake. So much so that one can understand the attitude of those who opted out and when it came to buying glass chose those elaborately cut modified versions of eighteenth-century styles.

Typical was the quilted satin effect achieved by trapping air (often in diamond patterns) between two layers of glass, the inner, opaque; the outer, colored and transparent. The outer surface was then treated with acid to give the final satin finish. Burmese glass, especially when used for the shades of oil lamps, was even more intriguing. Here, by means of localized heat control, yellow-greens merged into deep clouded pink in the same piece of glass.

Another late Victorian characteristic was the waving of the edges of objects. It is best seen in the more exotic oil lamps, but it applies equally to other things like bowls and vases which, with their rich colors and vegetable shapes, often look like hothouse plants. Sadly though, English glass of this period lacked the creative genius of a Lalique or of a Gallé. (Emile Gallé, the leading exponent of Art Nouveau in France, developed subtle colorings and a new technique combining clear and opaque glass ideally suited to the simple

'Clutha' glass vase designed by Christopher Dresser for James Couper & Sons of Glasgow in the late 1880's.

Layered glass vase with cut decoration by Emile Gallé, late 19th century

but flowing lines of Art Nouveau designs.) Ornate and extravagant as much late Victorian glass was, restraint had not been entirely abandoned. Some of the streaked and crackled 'Clutha' glass vases designed by Christopher Dresser for J. Couper & Sons of Glasgow have a quiet dignity. The same characteristic marks the work of Harry Powell. In the case of his early three-lipped ovoid decanter, its neck decorated with blue trailing, perhaps too much so. But no such subjugation of the creative force is apparent in his fragile long-stemmed wine glasses. His later work has a timeless quality, for it represents a perfect understanding of the medium, the result of a life-long study of the aims and achievements of glass makers of all nations and ages. If Tiffany's glass was the Art Nouveau of the emotions, Powell's was certainly that of the intellect.

Jewelry

The essential point to remember about jewelry is that, whatever its value, it is a fashion accessory rather than an independent work of art, and we are being remarkably illogical if we sneer at the more massive and complicated items of Victorian jewelry because they are not suited to the simpler cut of today's clothes. The enormous brooches and wide bracelets were designed to be worn with elaborate heavy dresses where anything smaller would have looked insignificant. To say that one does not like them is one thing, but to condemn them out of context as badly designed—any many people still do—is quite another.

I make this point not because I myself have a peculiar mission to preserve mid-Victorian jewelry, but because too often people call the unsuitable ugly, and then with a clear conscience destroy it. The more expensive pieces of Victorian jewelry suffered most from this attitude because there was the additional motive of the intrinsic value of the materials used. Diamonds were reset and gold was melted down and recast, and history is the poorer for it. Indeed, for this very reason there is a comparative shortage of the historically significant prestige items.

Gold bangle with light blue enamel and pearls, c. 1855

Small gold locket, mid-19th century

Fortunately for us (though not for the underpaid Victorian jeweler), conditions were such that craftsmanship was not restricted to these grand pieces, and the sheer quality of an item of Victorian jewelry that one can still buy for a few dollars is infinitely superior to what one would get for the same amount of money from a modern manufacturer.

The main reason for Victorian jewelry getting such comparatively low prices is that it was produced in such large quantity. This was not just simply because the Victorians liked pretty things; a bejeweled wife was also the ideal

Gold ring with diamonds and turquoises, c. 1855. A typical mid-Victorian setting

Early Victorian garnet and gold necklace

status symbol. The tradition of the *corbeille,* a sort of down-payment for a wife in the form of a gift of jewelry, which marked society weddings throughout the period, would certainly substantiate this point of view, especially since the contents of the most important *corbeilles* were described in detail by the gossip columnists of the day! The nineteenth century also saw the development of mass production in the making of jewelry, and the growth of Birmingham as a center of cheap ornaments. In the eighteenth century it was producing steel-cut and plated jewelry, but rapidly developed a whole range of inexpensive jewelry (which was within the reach of almost the poorest purse) and was soon exporting to Europe and the countries within the British Empire.

The eclecticism we have come to associate with Victorian applied art, in general, also marked the early period of Victorian jewelry. Apart from the native naturalistic style which developed from the revived Rococo, France, Germany, Scotland, Italy, even Nineveh, all provided stylistic inspiration, or at least ready-made jewelry which, if, like the cameo, it provided a success, could be copied by English craftsmen.

François-Desiré Froment-Meurice of Paris, for instance, produced magnificent Gothic bracelets and pendants which, though the originals are beyond the means of the normal collector, find their echoes in more modest pieces. At the other extreme, in terms of the value of the materials he used, was A. W. Pugin whose designs in the Gothic style included delicate jewelry in Berlin cast iron.

Nor was the baronial element lacking. The rather Scandinavian-looking Scottish jewelry of silver, set with cairngorms and pieces of polished stone, remained in fashion longer than it might otherwise have done, had it not been favored by the Queen herself, who was extremely fond of Scotland and things Scottish. Scotland probably also inspired the grouse-foot brooches. Like the more exotic gold-set tiger claws they symbolize the blood lust of the Victorian male.

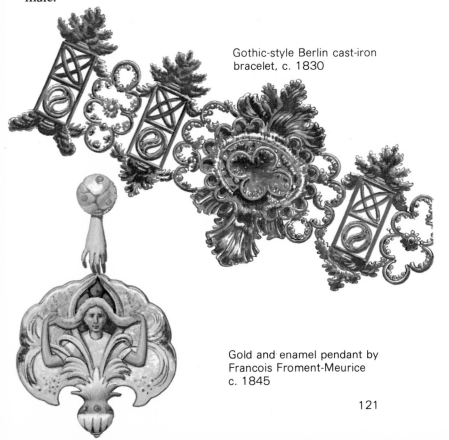

Gothic-style Berlin cast-iron bracelet, c. 1830

Gold and enamel pendant by Francois Froment-Meurice c. 1845

Going further afield, France supplied England with ivory costume jewelry, and Italy provided cameos, both shell and gem, though Paris came to be associated with the latter. Good shell cameos in gold settings are expensive, but occasionally one can find unset ones for a reasonable price. I recently bought the most perfect signed cameo I have seen outside a museum for about two dollars. It cost eleven dollars to set and the result has been valued at fifty to seventy-five dollars. Coral, either raw or made up into necklaces, tiaras, brooches and earrings also came from Italy, as did the mosaic and the cameo carved lava jewelry, both of which had a brief popularity.

More esoteric tastes were met by the Algerian and, as a result of the finds made at Nineveh, Assyrian style of jewelry.

Gold earrings with grape and tendril decoration, c. 1855

Convolvulus-shaped gold, turquoise and pearl brooch, c. 1850

Early Victorian cameo brooch with pinchbeck surround. The subject is the birth of Pallas Athene

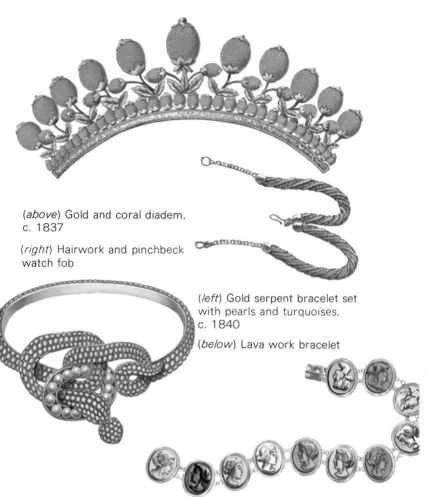

(*above*) Gold and coral diadem, c. 1837

(*right*) Hairwork and pinchbeck watch fob

(*left*) Gold serpent bracelet set with pearls and turquoïses, c. 1840

(*below*) Lava work bracelet

All these influences were eclipsed by the all-pervading naturalism. There were gold-set tiaras with coral berries, diamond roses, turquoise and pearl convolvulus, garnet and seed pearl grapes, and gold and enamel leaves. The Freudian snake bracelets and the later lizards, beetles and flies in glass represent a slightly sinister necrophilic sub-division of this category.

The necrophilic art *par excellence,* however, was hairwork either in the form of complete bracelets (or occasionally watch chains) of human hair or of delicately constructed patterns in rings, brooches and lockets.

If the subject of the sentiment was dead, the locket was often enameled black like the exquisite mourning rings it replaced. The mourning rings, lockets and brooches (the last two often contained a miniature portrait as well) are very popular today, but hairwork bracelets are less so. The reason for this is simple. In the one case we are actually touching part of a dead person, in the other there is no contact; for us death is as much of a taboo subject as sex was for the Victorians. But, as long as we do not have the same squeamish feelings about hair bracelets as we do about the members of some primitive societies wearing the bones of a dead wife or child, they can be very decorative.

Jet was another material widely used for mourning jewelry. However, in view of the enormous amounts produced, it is surprising how little survived. For those who could observe such niceties, amethysts were for half-mourning, which partly accounts for their popularity with the Victorians. Single-stone amethyst and pearl rings and single-strand amethyst necklaces are

Black-enameled gold mourning ring, c. 1840

Jet necklace, c. 1875

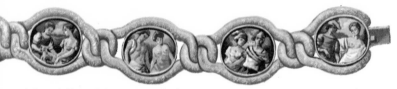

(*above*) Bracelet composed of enamel miniatures set in pinch-beck, c. 1845

(*below left*) Agate brooch in die-stamped gold surround

(*below right*) Brooch of peridots in die-stamped gold settings

among the most attractive examples of early Victorian jewelry. Other semi-precious stones particularly associated with the period were garnets, opals, topaz and turquoise. For large brooches, polished agate was often used.

The generally Rococo gold settings of most of the inexpensive items were die-stamped. This upsets the purists today, but it did mean that many more people were able to afford jewelry, and the dies themselves were usually so well cut (again the result of low wages) that the objection is really a compliment because it implies a direct comparison with the more expensive non-mass-produced article. Further down the scale of intrinsic value come pinchbeck and paste, both of which were again handled with the loving care reserved today for the most valuable materials. The use of pinchbeck declined rapidly after 1854 when it became legal to use lower carat golds in accordance with continental practice.

Necklet of gold, enamel and jewels, c. 1870

Ancient Etruscan and Renaissance jewelry represented the main external sources of inspiration for mid-Victorian jewelry. The former style is closely associated with Fortunato Pio Castellani who rediscovered the ancient technique of granulation. After his death, his son, Augusto, continued to produce skillful copies of Etruscan jewelry. Both the Castellanis and the Guiliano family produced copies and adaptations of Renaissance designs, but the irony here is that the perfection of their workmanship virtually destroys the impact of these pieces. The first thing one notices about genuine old jewelry are the slight imperfections. When these are absent, even the most complex handwork acquires the anonymity of the machine, and however perfect the copy may be in every other respect, it invariably lacks the spirit of the original.

Another far more elementary influence was making itself felt—sheer size. There were dangly fringed earrings, festoon necklaces, large cameos and enormous gold brooches and bracelets. Sometimes these had a little wire decoration around the edges and applique motifs in the middle or, alternatively,

Gold bangle with appliqué decoration, c. 1865

a star-shaped cluster of diamonds or small pearls around a central stone, or possibly enamel in some bright color. There was even a fashion for setting stones within stones.

Two things above all else account for the popularity of early Victorian jewelry: its youthful artlessness and the harmony achieved between the underlying structure and the subsequent decoration. The Rococo setting of a cameo brooch, for instance, was both structure and decoration. In late Victorian jewelry with its almost invisible mounts, decoration is emphasized at the cost of structure; in mid-Victorian jewelry the opposite holds true. In neither case is there the feeling of repose that is one of the traditional aims of art. With the large flat areas of mid-Victorian jewelry the division into basic structure on the one hand, and decoration on the other is very marked. Those designers who recognized

Renaissance-style pendant by
Castellani, c. 1868

Etruscan-style earrings by Giuliano,
c. 1870

127

Pearl dog collar
with silver and
paste bars, c. 1900

the problem and considered the design as a whole were inevitably more successful than those who—and contemporary critics were forever pointing out this fault—merely thought in terms of a flat surface on which to put a given amount of decoration. By the 1870's, however, the whole issue had been evaded by filling all flat areas with masses of busy engraving.

As far as minor fashions were concerned, jet grew in popularity, and was no longer restricted to mourning jewelry. Piqué work and the insect jewelry mentioned earlier were both in vogue.

The late 1870's and the 1880's witnessed a silver craze, and the heavy bangles, chains and lockets with all-over engraving dating from that time have been popular for years. But this, and most other jewelry fashions, came to an end in the 1880's. The aesthetes started the revolution by refusing to wear any jewelry at all, apart from the ubiquitous string of 'artist lady' beads. What began as a reaction to the machine-made and the garish caught on to such an extent that by the late 1880's no women of fashion wore jewelry in the daytime—with the exception of the occasional hat pin or small bar brooch. For formal occasions, like balls, jewelry was permitted, but only on condition it had no color: diamonds and pearls for those who could afford them; moonstones, opals and seed pearls for the rest.

As color was out, glitter was the goal. Diamonds arranged in invisible settings were worn in great clusters all over the body. On the head there would be a tiara or aigrette (a spray of jewels); around the neck would be a tight multistranded dog collar, then perhaps a stomacher on the bodice; diamond bows on the shoulders, rings and bracelets (the last two as fine as possible to give the illusion of naked jewels). Pearls were worn in dog collars and long knotted ropes.

Silver locket and
chain, early 1880's

Silver necklace given to
Jenny Lind by Queen
Victoria, c. 1880

Fortunately, more creative pieces were produced. From the mid-1880's onward C. R. Ashbee made Celtic-inspired jewelry, using mainly silver, amethyst, moonstone and rose quartz. The results were very similar in mood to his table silver. His more romantic pieces have the organic beauty of Art Nouveau without its undertones of Dorian Gray.

As with furniture, English Art Nouveau jewelry differed from its continental counterpart. In England, far more emphasis was placed on the use of metal, and the resulting designs are consequently more restrained than some of the *fin-de-siècle* fantasies of Lalique or the Fouquet-Mucha creations with their hothouse flowers, bats, snakes and female forms.

For those who cannot afford diamonds and pearls—and in any case, the late Victorian jewelers treated them both in

Gold and enamel brooch set with a star sapphire by C. R. Ashbee, c. 1892

Typical gold and glass brooch by René Lalique, 1903

an unenterprising way—there is really very little to collect apart from silver and the jewelry in the Arts and Crafts and Art Nouveau tradition. Late Victorian châtelaines, if one is lucky enough to come across them, can be lovely, and small silver watches, silver belt buckles and cloak clasps are still surprisingly cheap. Some of the hat pins, too, are charming, but the bar brooches (often with a heart motif), the sporting brooches (golf clubs) ·and the innumerable novelty brooches (trains, pickaxes) are a matter of taste. Toward the end of the century, little animal brooches came into fashion, and have been made ever since, but I think they have neither charm nor merit. On the whole, the earlier periods provide a better hunting ground.

Brooch of enamel, gold, sapphire and topaz set *en cabochon*, designed by E. Grasset, 1900. The link with poster design is self-evident

Gold, diamond and turquoise cockerel brooch, c. 1895

Embroidery and needlework

In Victorian middle-class society, in general, and in early Victorian society, in particular, the woman's place was in the home. An independent career was unthinkable, not only because the man's comfort was the woman's career, but also because if the wife worked, it would be automatically assumed that she had to work—with the consequent loss of status for the husband. So, the wife organized the servants—and even a modest household had its complement of these—played the piano, read something improving, or embroidered.

Berlinwork, which required little skill other than the ability to hold a needle and to follow a pattern, stitch by stitch, overwhelms all other early and mid-Victorian needlework by volume, if not by creative worth. The subjects themselves are roughly what one would expect: flowers, religious scenes, scenes from the novels of Sir Walter Scott, sentimental rustic scenes (as in some transfer-printed plates), and representations of the Royal Family, with or without dogs. Classical and Renaissance subjects came into fashion in the 1860's and 1870's. However, by the 1880's Berlinwork had almost completely been replaced by art needlework.

Berlinwork panel of the Prince of Wales, c. 1845

Needlework picture with hatband, c. 1870, embroidered by a sailor

The earlier examples are generally more mellow than the later which sometimes included beadwork. Some of the panels were framed and displayed as separate works of art; others were used as chairbacks or for more mundane purposes such as decorating the lord and master's slippers.

A considerable number of Berlinwork copies of famous paintings were also made, but I find them less satisfying than other forms of needlework picture. These ranged from the naive woolwork representations of sailing ships (usually the work of the sailors themselves) to fantastically detailed copies of etchings and paintings.

Much more creative than any amount of laborious filling-in of Berlinwork patterns, and often equally time-consuming (for those to whom this represents a cardinal virtue) were the patchwork coverlets (patchwork was also used to decorate smaller items like smoking caps). Here the choice of color and design, which could be figurative, geometric or a combination of both, was much more that of the individual, and the results are often exquisite. As for quilting itself, it was becoming more of a rural industry than a common pastime. Its strongholds were northern England and South Wales.

Some of the early and late Victorian ribbonwork is pretty in a Frenchified way, but the more ingenious methods of imitating fruit and flowers in fabric are usually of greater interest to the sociologist.

Children's samplers were usually in cross-stitch and they were less popular in the second half of the period than the first. Even more of a dying art was the elaborate stitching of laborer's smocks.

Broderie anglaise, in contrast, was gaining ground rapidly, and Mountmellick-work in heavy white thread on a cotton satin base was also popular for larger items. The embroidery by hand of such things as christening robes was organized on semi-industrial lines, but by the 1850's the future of the art was being threatened by the embroidery machine invented in 1828. By the 1870's Swiss machines could do any kind of embroidery.

For the needlework revival of the 1860's onward we have to thank architects like A. W. Pugin and G. E. Street and, once again, William Morris. The architects became interested in ecclesiastical vestments in the course of their work, and soon

Silk on wool sampler by Emma Susanna Matthew, 1839

White homespun linen wedding smock from Sussex, mid-19th century

134

Part of an embroidery frieze designed by Edward Burne-Jones and William Morris, 1874–82

ecclesiastical embroidery was being produced by a number of needlework societies—as well as by Morris & Co. Morris's own interest in embroidery dates from the late 1850's, and his designs combine the romantic medievalism of his painted furniture with the vigorous naturalism of his wallpaper and fabric patterns.

After the success of the Royal School of Art Needlework which was founded in 1872, a number of similar organizations were established. Earlier techniques were revived, and art needlework was as widely practiced as Berlin woolwork had been before. Apart from copies of old designs, Japanese and Renaissance subjects were very popular. The work itself was often of extremely high quality, but still to some extent bounded by the mechanical approach inherent in working to a predetermined design.

For more spontaneous work we have to wait for Jessie Newbery and Ann Macbeth of the Glasgow School of Art. Ann Macbeth maintained that 'the design and stitchery should arise naturally out of the technique itself' (B. Morris, *Victorian Embroidery,* page 157). This concept was of particular importance from an educational point of view because it radically altered the teaching of needlework to children as a school subject.

Metalwork

The Victorians lived in an age of cast iron. They built bridges with it; some of them slept on it, and others were buried in it in a futile attempt to foil the body snatchers.

> They burst the patent coffin first,
> And they cut through the lead:
> And they laugh'd aloud when they saw the shroud,
> Because they had got at the dead.
>
> (Robert Southey, *The Surgeon's Warning*)

Cast-iron mort safes were a minority taste, but every Victorian house had its cast-iron kitchen range and its cast-iron fireplaces. The latter are still being torn out to be replaced by the modern tiled variety. In case you are ever confronted with the problem of reversing the process, you can buy one for a very reasonable price at auctions.

Along with the fireplace went cast-iron or brass firedogs, brass fenders, copper or brass helmet-shaped coal buckets and brass fire irons. The coal buckets have been in

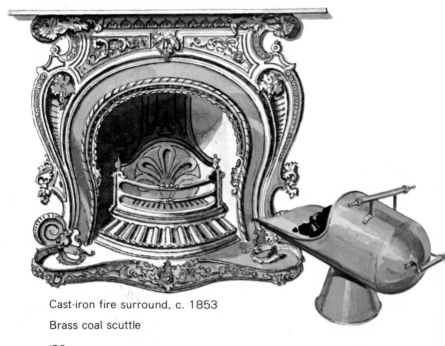

Cast-iron fire surround, c. 1853

Brass coal scuttle

demand for some time. Brass fenders too are quite popular, especially those with an Art Nouveau flavor. Brass fire irons and firedogs, however, vary enormously in price. Generally speaking, if they are bought from a shop that emphasizes their decorative aspect, they are expensive, whereas in a second-hand shop they are simply functional objects which, with the growth of central heating, have less and less of a function to fulfill.

On the mantelpieces were bronze figures, or cheaper versions in spelter (zinc). As with door porters, brass was also occasionally used. The Marly Horses are by far the most common subject, and most junk shops have a pair for six dollars or so. Figures symbolizing Truth, the electric telegraph or some other wonder of the age ran a close second in popularity. The large bronzes of torch-bearing ladies have long since been bought and converted into standard lamps. Spelter (the price of which has recently risen steeply) was also used for massive Renaissance-type vases and ewers, and for the surrounds of large clocks.

Brass and steel fire irons

Late Victorian spelter figure

On the walls in many Victorian homes there used to be bronze gaslight fittings, and sometimes, in a corner, a palatial brass cage for the parrot. Further discreet glitter was provided by brass cornice poles and brass curtain rings and, on the doors, brass finger plates. The front door usually had a handsome knocker either in brass or cast iron.

Cast-iron money boxes and the more decorative cast-iron door porters have been collected for some time. In the case of the money boxes, it is interesting to note that, if anything, the prices have gone down in the last year or so. Perhaps this is because they were rather unattractively adorned, for example a face, rolling the whites of his eyes as he swallows the money put into his hand. Taste has become too refined to appreciate that sort of thing.

Cast-iron oil stoves, umbrella stands, tables, chairs and garden seats, on the other hand, have only really come into vogue in the last few years. Although the prices asked in antique shops for garden furniture are high enough to warrant modern reproductions in aluminum,

Copper mold

Copper kettle

Brass bird cage

they can still occasionally be found in the country at reasonable prices. But then, of course, one is faced with transport costs. In any case, a sewing machine stand with a marble top often makes a good alternative to a small table.

The Victorians also made furniture in strip brass. This was rare at the time and is rarer now. The beds are interesting, yet not outstanding, but the strip-brass rocker, very similar in overall effect to the bentwood rocking chair, is delightful.

The Victorian kitchen, however, provides more attractive metal objects than the rest of the house put together. In the early part of the period, copper cooking utensils predominated. There were copper molds, kettles, measures, scoops and saucepans. A glance at the rows and rows of these implements in the kitchens gives us some idea of how hard the one using them must have had to work.

Copper looks lovely, but before buying a battery of Victorian copper saucepans it is worth considering the practical problems that will arise. If they are for use, then

Cast-iron table and garden seat

they will probably have to be retinned and that means extra expense. If they are just for show, there is still the cleaning problem. One can lacquer them, but I think that takes the warmth out of the metal. In the 1850's enameled cast iron began to replace tinned copper in the kitchen. Though these pots have a certain massive presence, it in no way compares with the bright glow of polished copper.

Pewter was used in the kitchen and the public house throughout the period, and many of the designs of the pots and measures are in the eighteenth-century tradition. Victorian ale mugs are still relatively cheap and tend to be scorned by collectors in the same way that Victorian furniture was at one time. With Art Nouveau, as we have seen, pewter became a fashionable metal once again. It was also used throughout the Victorian period for small items like inkwells.

Japanned wares (lacquered work) with varying amounts of decoration were produced throughout the Victorian period, but earlier examples are usually better. Japanned hat boxes, in particular, with their discreet gilt initials and decorative bands are very pleasing objects.

The popularity of brass candlesticks and, even more, of brass scales can be linked with that of stripped pine. As for brass lamps, they are so popular that reproductions are flooding the market, and the trade seems to be switching its attention to the cast-iron variety with wavy-edged shades.

When we come to such established favorites as hunting

Post office scales with excise stamp of 1868

Two typical Victorian horse brasses—crescent and bell shape

horns, horse brasses, warming pans and carriage lamps, copies far outnumber originals, and if one cannot tell at a glance which is which, any specialist book on the subject will give a list of points to look for. With horse brasses, for instance, if the back is left pitted and lumpy, it is almost certainly a product of the souvenir trade.

Finally, for those who have the room, the wrought iron, or occasionally brass, ornamental brackets of defunct shop signs provide excellent examples of Victorian craftsmanship at a minimal cost. I suppose the ingenious can rig them up as lamps, but I think a collection mounted on a white wall would look infinitely better. Indeed, a well-arranged collection of almost any type of object can look attractive when presented in this way.

Oil carriage lamp, c. 1889

Pewter tankard

Bric-à-brac and miscellaneous

In the short space available, all one can hope to do is to bring to the notice of the potential collector a selection of the more interesting objects that fall outside the main categories dealt with so far.

Possibly the most extensive group of all consists of small objects either made of silver or decorated with silver. Favorites among these are silver pocket watches: large heavy ones for men and daintier versions with decorative faces for women. These often cost little more than the scrap value of the metal itself. The same can be said of the countless silver-topped bottles which, together with silver-backed mirrors and hair brushes, once formed elegant toilet sets. Snuff boxes and other small silver boxes, sovereign cases, and visiting card cases (also made of mother-of-pearl set in a diamond pattern) are equally attractive. Perhaps

(*top left*) Late Victorian lady's silver watch

(*top right*) Silver-topped bottle from a traveling toilet set

(*right*) Small brass-topped inkwell from a traveling writing box

142

most widely collected of all, though, are the silver and the rarer ceramic wine labels.

Almost as numerous as the different types of small silver objects are the various items associated with letter writing. There are inkwells, paperweights, paperknives, letter racks and, of course, the writing box itself which opens out to form a sloping desk. The lower portion of it contains pens, inkwells and, almost without fail, a secret drawer. These can be located by checking that the internal measurements plus the thickness of the wood come to the same as the external measurements. If not, a few minutes careful tapping and prodding should reveal a spring—and, who knows, you might find something. I never have, but my wife once found a newspaper clipping proclaiming the relief of Mafeking in the Union of South

(*top left*) Visiting card case in mother-of-pearl

(*top right*) Late Victorian sherry bottle label

(*right*) Traveling dressing case, 1862

143

(*top left*) Mid-Victorian glass
dome with wax flower decoration

(*top right*) Box decorated
with shells, c. 1880

(*right*) Ivory dress fan, c. 1867

Africa. The earlier boxes are usually brass-bound like
military chests; later versions have mother-of-pearl inlay,
and both types have sunken brass handles.

But if one finds these are too bulky to collect, no such
problem should arise with ornamental buttons (I have a
splendid set of silver livery buttons), fans or those egg-
shaped things called hand coolers by the romantic and
sock darners by the prosaic. I expect both factions are
right. The eggs themselves can be of stone, glass, porcelain or pottery, sometimes colored to look like actual
birds' eggs.

The same desire to deceive is illustrated by Victorian

Glass case with butterfly specimens, c. 1890

wax flowers and fruit. The flowers have not held up as well, but the fruit can be remarkably realistic. The desire to trap Nature in a glass case and to make it everlasting was a strong Victorian theme. Paper or wax or dried flowers, stuffed animals, birds and fish brought Nature into the sitting room, but in a very tidy, tamed and artificial way.

For a lover of the unsophisticated arts, the Victorian era provides a wide choice. Examples of amateur chip carving, poker work, straw marquetry, shell, cork and beadwork are fairly common. Less common are breadwork (moistened bread being used as a modeling material) and fish-scale or beetle-wing embroidery, although I except even these have their experts. For sheer craftsmanship, however, what can surpass a good ship in a bottle or some other

Late Victorian case with pike

sailor's love token like a spoon on a chain all carved out of the same piece of wood? (this, incidentally, is probably the origin of 'to spoon').

Continuing on the romantic theme, an increasing number of people collect Victorian valentine cards, postcards and Christmas cards. The last of these I think are the most interesting because they give a particularly good insight into Victorian attitudes. Dead birds are a favorite subject. One printed about 1880 shows a robin with its feet in the air and the following macabre mottoes: 'Sweet messenger of calm decay and Peace Divine' and 'But peaceful was the night, wherein the Prince of Light, His reign of peace upon the

Model of the Cutty Sark in a bottle

earth began'. Even more peculiar is W. S. Coleman's 'The Bathers' which shows a semi-nude thirteen-year-old girl in a river. Harmless enough one might think, but the description in the trade catalogue puts a different emphasis on the matter:

> A tripping, fair, light-hearted girl,
> Not yet the ripened woman quite.

It does not need a psychiatrist to link this with the Victorian vice of child prostitution.

(*left*) Typical envelope or sachet card. This would have been scented.
(*right*) Late Victorian valentine card, made from layers of die-stamped paper.
(*below*) Christmas card of 1860's

Also in a popular idiom are the numerous Baxter prints (made by a sophisticated version of the process F. & R. Pratt used for their printed pot lids), sporting prints, music covers, posters and advertisements (often incorporating the Royal Family). But fascinating as many of these undoubtedly are, they do not bear comparison with the achievements of Victorian photography. Even a colliery group photograph has a dignity and a sense of occasion wholly lacking in most of today's photographs. When it comes to individual portraits, how many present-day photographers can equal the work of Margaret Cameron? Her uncanny talent for drawing out the essential personality of her sitters has rarely been rivaled.

Cast-iron picture frame

Early cameras, ironically, are more highly valued than the photographs they produced but, with their brass-cased lenses and polished mahogany bodies, they are certainly very attractive. And so are the magic lanterns, old street lamps, musical boxes, early gramophones, telescopes, sextants, microscopes and other scientific instruments which figure so

Lithochrome illustration, c. 1880

148

(*right*) Victorian soap advertisement

(*left*) Early Victorian sextant

(*below*) Late 19th-century magic lantern

Victorian lettering
for a tavern

(*below*) Lettering for
a shop window

prominently in interior design magazines. Gilt, copper, brass and enamel shop lettering is a more recent arrival on the collecting scene.

Fire marks, on the other hand, are an established favorite. Originally each insurance company had its own fire brigade, and they only put out fires in the houses they themselves insured. For easy recognition, a fire mark consisting of the appropriate company symbol, and often the number of the policy as well, would be displayed on the outside of the house. By the time Victoria came to the throne the separate services had amalgamated, and fire marks merely served as advertisements.

Another form of advertisement, the inn sign, has received, I think, almost more attention than it deserves. The best examples are superb, but often the original has been so extensively restored that it reminds one of the roadsweeper who said he had used the same brush for ten years and that now he was on his twentieth head and third handle.

Much more interesting are the traditional forms of decoration to be seen on narrow boats, gypsy caravans and in fairgrounds. The recent revival of interest in narrow boats and in the stagnating canals of England has meant that many a barge is now bright again with a profusion of roses and castles and all kinds of vivid designs. Roundabout horses, the best of fairground art, can occasionally be found in antique shops, but at a price. Gypsy caravans are expensive—a very good price being from $1,200 to $1,450. They are beautifully painted and carved and ingeniously fitted out, though the bunks are usually too short for those above average height. Those with more sophisticated tastes (and even larger purses) might well consider a Victorian carriage instead. The less ambitious can acquire a Victorian pram (their designs varied from miniature chariots and carriages to the more conventional shape which continues today)

Landau-type perambulator, 1876

151

'Ariel' penny farthing, 1870

or a penny farthing. The bicycle had an enormous effect
on Victorian society. For the first time the badly paid clerk
or factory girl was able to go where he or she liked at a minimal cost. It brought freedom of movement (something
that until then had been the prerogative of the rich) within
the reach of the majority. It even affected the design of
clothes, creating a functional style suited to the robust 'sport'
of bicycling.

Swords and firearms have always had their devotees, but
I find it very difficult to see why anyone should want to
collect truncheons, but even these have attracted the eye of
the collector.

A current craze that I can more readily understand is that
for Victorian toys, the majority of which were made in
Germany. In the Victorian era, Germany enjoyed much the

English rocking horse,
early 19th century

Jigging Irishman
toy, c. 1850

same reputation as Japan in more recent years. Particularly
sought after are automata and toys based on scientific prin-
ciples like the gyroscope, originally used to demonstrate the
rotation of the earth.

Less sophisticated, but perhaps most popular of all because
of its universal appeal, is the rocking horse. A large Victorian
one can easily cost $150, but it is a beautiful thing, com-
bining convincing realism with a simplicity of design dictated
by the necessary shape of the toy.

Policeman's truncheon, late Victorian rifle, ceremonial sword and
bayonet

153

Victorian dolls, too, are very much in fashion, and rightly so because they are equally well made, having perfectly modeled porcelain heads, real hair and clothes correct in every detail.

Attention to detail is also the chief characteristic of the more elaborate types of doll's house. By studying them, one can get an excellent overall impression of a typical upper-middle-class Victorian house. Fixtures and fittings, pots, pans, crockery, furniture—everything is a perfect miniature of the real thing.

Many of the pieces of miniature furniture one comes across, however, were designed for a more serious purpose: as samples for traveling salesmen. At one time these items were thought to be apprentices' test pieces, but there is little evidence for this belief. But apprentices did sometimes make those Gothic-looking skeleton clocks which are usually covered by a protective glass dome. The theory was that the apprentice should prove his ability by making a complete clock himself, right down to the last screw.

The above is, of course, only a fraction of many other small but interesting Victorian items available to the collector.

BOOKS TO READ

For further reading on this subject, the following titles are recommended and are usually available at bookstores and public libraries.

1897 Sears Roebuck Catalogue. Reprinted by Chelsea House, 1968.

The New Antiques: Knowing and Buying Victorian Furniture. George Grotz. Doubleday, 1963.

The Early Victorian Period, 1830–1860. Ralph Edwards and Leonard Ramsey(eds.). London: The Connoisseur, 1958.

Decorative Art of the Victorian Era. Frances Lichter. Bonanza Books, 1950.

Victorian Comfort. John Gloag. London: A. & C. Black, 1961.

Victorian Taste. John Gloag. London: A. & C. Black, 1962.

The Victorian Home. Ralph Dutton. London: Batsford, 1954.

Art Nouveau. Mario Amaya. London: Studio Vista, 1966.

Collecting Victoriana. Mary Peter. London: Arco, 1965.

Collecting Antiques on a Small Income. Geoffrey Beard. London: Hutchinson, 1957.

Victorian Furniture. F. G. Roe. London: Phoenix House, 1952.

Victorian Furniture. R. W. Symonds and B. B. Whineray. London: Country Life, 1962.

Victorian Silver and Silver-Plate. Patricia Wardle. London: Herbert Jenkins, 1963.

Victorian Porcelain. G. A. Godden. London: Herbert Jenkins, 1961.

Victorian Pottery. Hugh Wakefield. London: Herbert Jenkins, 1962.

Victorian Jewellery. Margaret Flower. London: Cassell, 1951.

Victorian Embroidery. Barbara Morris. London: Herbert Jenkins, 1962.

Children's Toys Throughout the Ages. Leslie Daiken. London: Spring Books, 1963.

The History of the Christmas Card. George Buday. London: Spring Books, 1964.

A Book of Dolls and Doll Houses. Flora Gill Jacobs and Estrid Faurholt. Rutland: Charles E. Tuttle, 1967.

Victorian Household. M. Lockhead. Hillary.

Victorian Glass. R. W. Lee. Wellesley Hills: Lee Publications.

Victoriana. J. Laver. Hawthorn.

Victoriana, a Collector's Guide. V. Wood. Macmillan.

INDEX

OTHER TITLES IN THE SERIES

The GROSSET ALL-COLOR GUIDES provide a library of authoritative information for readers of all ages. Each comprehensive text with its specially designed illustrations yields a unique insight into a particular area of man's interests and culture.

NOW AVAILABLE

PREHISTORIC ANIMALS
BIRD. BEHAVIOR
WILD CATS
FOSSIL MAN
PORCELAIN
MILITARY UNIFORMS 1686–1918
BIRDS OF PREY
FLOWER ARRANGING
MICROSCOPES & MICROSCOPIC LIFE
THE PLANT KINGDOM
ROCKETS & MISSILES
FLAGS OF THE WORLD
ATOMIC ENERGY
WEATHER & WEATHER FORECASTING
TRAINS
SAILING SHIPS & SAILING CRAFT
ELECTRONICS
MYTHS & LEGENDS OF ANCIENT GREECE
CATS, HISTORY—CARE—BREEDS
DISCOVERY OF AFRICA
HORSES & PONIES
FISHES OF THE WORLD
ASTRONOMY
SNAKES OF THE WORLD
DOGS, SELECTION—CARE—TRAINING
MAMMALS OF THE WORLD
VICTORIAN FURNITURE AND FURNISHINGS
MYTHS & LEGENDS OF ANCIENT EGYPT
COMPUTERS AT WORK
GUNS